MIDDLE EAST NATIONS IN THE NEWS

Iraq
IN THE NEWS

PAST, PRESENT, AND FUTURE

Wim Coleman and Pat Perrin

MyReportLinks.com Books

an imprint of

Enslow Publishers, Inc.

Box 398, 40 Industrial Road
Berkeley Heights, NJ 07922
USA

Library of Congress Cataloging-in-Publication Data

Coleman, Wim.
  Iraq in the news : past, present, and future / Wim Coleman and Pat Perrin.
    p. cm.—(Middle East nations in the news)
  Includes bibliographical references and index.
  ISBN 1-59845-027-1
  1. Iraq—Juvenile literature. I. Perrin, Pat. II. Title. III. Series.
  DS70.62.C65 2006
  956.7—dc22

                         2005032462

Printed in the United States of America

10 9 8 7 6 5 4 3 2 1

To Our Readers:
Through the purchase of this book, you and your library gain access to the Report Links that specifically back up this book.
The Publisher will provide access to the Report Links that back up this book and will keep these Report Links up to date on **www.myreportlinks.com** for five years from the book's first publication date.
We have done our best to make sure all Internet addresses in this book were active and appropriate when we went to press. However, the author and the Publisher have no control over, and assume no liability for, the material available on those Internet sites or on other Web sites they may link to.
The usage of the MyReportLinks.com Books Web site is subject to the terms and conditions stated on the Usage Policy Statement on **www.myreportlinks.com.**
A password may be required to access the Report Links that back up this book. The password is found on the bottom of page 4 of this book.
Any comments or suggestions can be sent by e-mail to comments@myreportlinks.com or to the address on the back cover.

Photo Credits: AP/Wide World Photos, pp. 1, 85; Central Intelligence Agency, p. 6; © BBC MMVI, pp. 49, 78; © BBC 2005, pp. 9, 37; © Corel Corporation, pp. 21, 28, 31, 35, 39, 41, 48, 66; © 1996–2006 United Nations, p. 92; © 1997–2006 Arabic-Media.com, p. 75; © The British Museum, p. 63; © 2000 The British Museum, p. 64; © 2000–2005 GlobalSecurity.org, p. 24; © 2001–06 Iran Chamber Society, p. 86; © 2002 Arab.net: Iraq, p. 17; © 2002–06 WGBH, p. 45; © 2003 Iraq Ministry of Foreign Affairs, p. 103; © 2005 Cable News Network, LP, LLLP, p. 96; © 2005 ESPN Internet Ventures, p. 57; © 2005 The American-Israeli Cooperative Enterprise, p. 60; © 2006 Cable News Network, LP, LLLP, p. 11; © 2006 MacNeil/Lehrer Productions, p. 111; © 2006 WN Network, p. 102; Enslow Publishers, Inc., p. 5; Library of Congress, pp. 43, 71; MiddleEastUK.com, p. 50; Minnesota State University, p. 26; MyReportLinks.com Books, p. 4; Photos.com, pp. 23, 59; The White House, p. 55; United Nations Global Teaching and Learning Project, p. 90; University of Pennsylvania Museum of Archaeology and Anthropology, p. 68; University of Texas Libraries, pp. 8, 14, 81; U.S. Department of Defense, pp. 3, 12, 18, 53, 88, 99, 105, 109; U.S. Department of State, pp. 32, 72.

Cover Photo: AP/Wide World Photos

Cover Description: Former Iraqi leader: Saddam Hussein, on trial for crimes against humanity.

Contents

Disabled Iraqi tank

Iraqi voter

MyReportLinks.com Books
Great Books, Great Links, Great for Research!

The Internet sites featured in this book can save you hours of research time. These Internet sites—we call them **"Report Links"**—are constantly changing, but we keep them up to date on our Web site.

When you see this "Approved Web Site" logo, you will know that we are directing you to a great Internet site that will help you with your research.

Give it a try! Type http://www.myreportlinks.com into your browser, click on the series title and enter the password, then click on the book title, and scroll down to the Report Links listed for this book.

The Report Links will bring you to great source documents, photographs, and illustrations. MyReportLinks.com Books save you time, feature Report Links that are kept up to date, and make report writing easier than ever! A complete listing of the Report Links can be found on pages 112–113 at the back of the book.

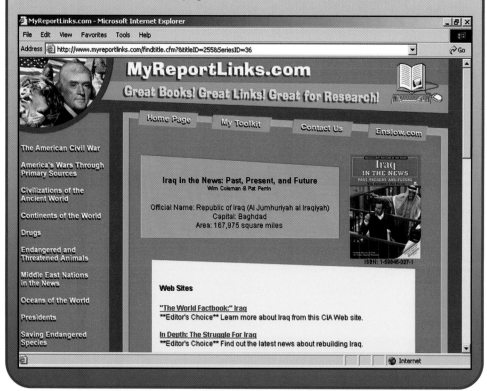

Please see "To Our Readers" on the copyright page for important information about this book, the MyReportLinks.com Web site, and the Report Links that back up this book.

Please enter NIQ1010 if asked for a password.

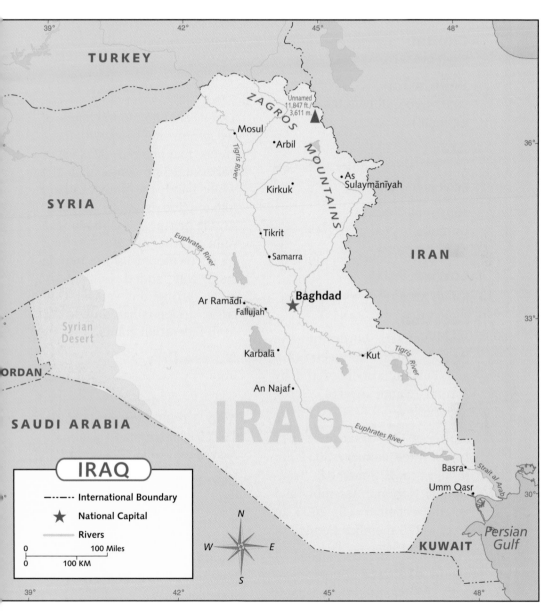

▲ *A map of present-day Iraq.*

Iraq Facts

Official Name
Republic of Iraq
(Al Jumhuriyah al Iraqiyah)

Capital
Baghdad

Population
26,074,906 (July 2005 estimate)

Area
167,975 square miles (435,055 kilometers)

Highest Point
Unnamed peak, 11,847 feet (3,611 meters)

Lowest Point
Persian Gulf at 0 feet

Location
Middle East, bordering the Persian Gulf, between Iran and Kuwait, also bordered by Jordan, Saudi Arabia, Syria, and Turkey.

Type of Government
Iraqis voted January 30, 2005 to elect a 275-member Transitional National Assembly and voted December 15, 2005 to elect a 275-member Council of Representatives.

Head of State
Iraqi Transitional Government (ITG) President Jalal Talabani

Head of Government
Prime Minister Designate Jawad al-Maliki

Monetary Unit
New Iraqi dinar (NID)

Official Languages
Arabic, Kurdish (official in Kurdish regions), Assyrian, Armenian

Flag
Three equal horizontal bands of red, white, and black with three green five-pointed stars in a horizontal line centered in the white band; the phrase Allahu Akbar (God is great) in green Arabic script (Allahu to the right of the middle star and Akbar to the left of the middle star) was added in January 1991 during the Persian Gulf crisis; design is based upon the Arab Liberation colors.

Nationality
Iraqi

Ethnic Groups
Arab 75–80 percent, Kurdish 15–20 percent, Turkoman, Assyrian or other 5 percent

Life Expectancy
68.7 years

Religion
Muslim 97 percent (Shi'a 60–65 percent, Sunni 32–37 percent), Christian or other 3 percent

National Holiday
The Iraqi Interim Government has yet to declare a new national holiday.[1]

Time Line

1918 —Ottoman Empire falls and Iraq is under a British mandate.

1921 —*Aug. 23:* Faisal becomes the first king of Iraq.

1932 —*Oct. 3:* Iraq gains complete independence from Great Britain.

1933 —Faisal dies and his son, Ghazi, becomes king.

1934–
1939 —Iraqi government changes hands many times over five years because of military coups. Ghazi is merely a figurehead leader.

1939 —Faisal II becomes king, but since he is so young, Emir Abd al-Ilah rules as a regent.

1945 —After World War II, Iraq becomes a member of the Arab League.

1948 —Iraq participates in unsuccessful Arab-Israeli War against Israel.

1958 —Military coup overthrows the Iraqi monarchy. General Abdul Karim Kassem declares Iraq a republic and becomes its leader.

1963 —Ba'ath party takes over the Iraqi government temporarily, but Colonel Abd al Salam Aref takes back control.

1968 —Ba'ath party leader Ahmad Hasan al-Bakr overthrows Aref.

1973 —Iraq fights in unsuccessful Yom Kippur War against Israel.

1979 —*July 16:* Saddam Hussein gains power in Iraq.

1980–
1988 —Iran-Iraq War ends without a clear winner. A total of 1.5 million people die.

1990 —Iraq invades neighboring country of Kuwait.

1991 —*Jan. to April:* Iraq is defeated in the Persian Gulf War fought to regain Kuwaiti independence.

2003 —*March 19:* President George W. Bush declares war on Iraq. His "coalition of the willing" launches Operation Iraqi Freedom. The United States and Great Britain are the leaders of the coalition.

May 1: Bush declares that major combat operations in Iraq are over. Insurgency begins.

Dec. 13: Deposed Iraqi leader Saddam Hussein is captured from his hiding place. He is jailed to be put on trial for war crimes.

2005 —*Jan. 30:* Iraqi people vote to elect a 275-member transitional national assembly.

Oct. 15: Iraqis vote to approve a new constitution.

Dec. 15: Iraqi people vote to elect a 275-member council of representatives which will be the first parliament.

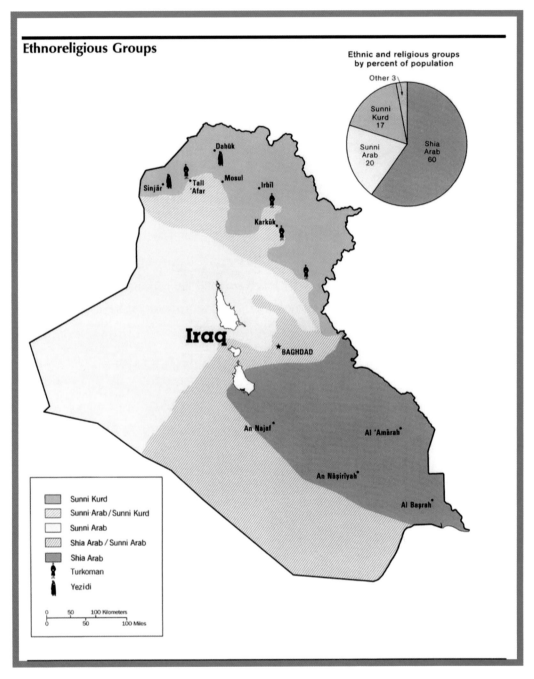

Ethnoreligious Groups

Ethnic and religious groups by percent of population

Other 3

Sunni Kurd 17

Sunni Arab 20

Shia Arab 60

Dahūk

Mosul

Sinjār

Tall 'Afar

Irbīl

Karkūk

Iraq

BAGHDAD

An Najaf

Al 'Amārah

An Nāşirīyah

Al Başrah

Sunni Kurd

Sunni Arab / Sunni Kurd

Sunni Arab

Shia Arab / Sunni Arab

Shia Arab

Turkoman

Yezidi

0   50   100 Kilometers
0   50   100 Miles

This map shows the regions where the people of different sects of Islam and ethnicities live in Iraq.

Chapter 1 ▶

Iraq in the News

On January 30, 2005, Sabria Sharif Mohammed awoke early in the morning full of hope. Iraq's first free election in fifty years was scheduled for that day, and she was eager to exercise her right to vote.

Mohammed belongs to an ethnic group called the Kurds that had suffered terribly under the

Vivian Salem Mate's family was killed while they fled from fighting in Baghdad. Many Iraqis like her and Sabria Sharif Mohammed have suffered losses since the start of Operation Iraqi Freedom. View more images at **In Depth: The Struggle for Iraq.**

Iraqi dictatorship of Saddam Hussein. Now that Hussein had been overthrown, a better life seemed to lie ahead for the Kurdish people. But Sabria knew that a better life depended upon a stable democracy, and that it was her civic duty to go to the polls that day.

Before she left her home, Mohammed sent her sixteen-year-old youngest son, Youssef, to fetch water from the neighborhood pump. A few minutes later, Youssef was struck by a mortar bomb and killed.

Grief stricken, Sabria bathed her son's body and wrapped him in a shroud. After she made arrangements for his burial, she walked three miles to the polls, weeping all the way. There she voted, just as she had planned to do when she woke up that morning. Her terrible tragedy added to her determination to help make an Iraqi democracy possible.[1]

Mohammed was not the only Iraqi to show great courage that day. Millions of Iraqis risked their lives going to the polls to vote. Via television and other media, the whole world watched as Iraq took its first major step toward democracy.

A dictator, Saddam Hussein, ruled Iraq with an iron hand from 1979 until 2003. In 2003, armed forces led by the United States and Great Britain invaded Iraq and overthrew Hussein's regime. Iraq was at long last liberated from its tyrant—but it was still not free, and certainly not at peace. Hussein's government was scarcely gone before a major insurgency, or armed rebellion, began.

As the elections of January 30, 2005 approached, violence intensified. The rebels sought to destroy the democratic process. On January 23, a disturbing audio recording was posted on the Internet. It was supposedly spoken by Abu Musab al-Zarqawi, an Iraq-based leader of the international terrorist organization al-Qaeda.

"We have declared a fierce war on this evil principle of democracy and those who follow this wrong ideology," the recording said. "Anyone who tries to help set up this system is part of it. . . .

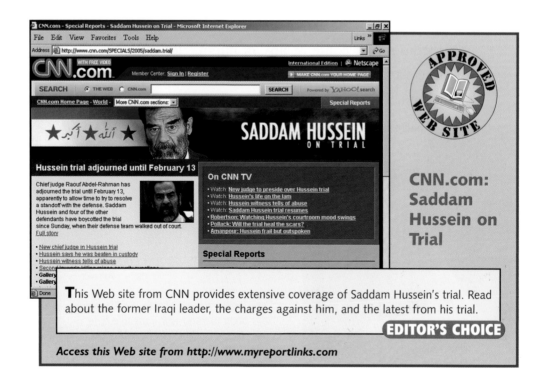

CNN.com: Saddam Hussein on Trial

This Web site from CNN provides extensive coverage of Saddam Hussein's trial. Read about the former Iraqi leader, the charges against him, and the latest from his trial.

EDITOR'S CHOICE

Access this Web site from http://www.myreportlinks.com

Candidates in elections are seeking to become demi-gods while those who vote for them are infidels."[2] Insurgents also spread leaflets threatening voters. "We vow to wash the streets of Baghdad with the voters' blood," one leaflet announced.[3]

Although the streets were not truly "washed with blood" on January 30, forty-four Iraqis were killed by insurgent attacks that day. One brave policeman is said to have dragged a suicide bomber away from a crowded polling station. Only the policeman and the bomber died when the explosive was set off.[4]

The courage of millions of other Iraqis on that day was astonishing. Many waited in lines at the polls for an hour, fully aware that an insurgent strike might come at any moment.[5] By the end of the day, more than 8.5 million Iraqis had voted— about 58 percent of those registered to vote.[6]

The January 2005 elections were not intended to create a final democratic

◁ The index finger of this Iraqi man has been marked with indelible blue ink. This was done to prove that he voted in Iraq's first-ever national election held January 30, 2005.

government, however. Their more limited purpose was to elect a body of representatives to write a new Iraqi constitution. The Iraqi people voted again on October 15, 2005, and chose to accept the constitution.

Nevertheless, Iraq remains troubled and divided. The United States- and British-led coalition cannot occupy the country forever. But what will become of Iraq after coalition forces leave? Can Iraqis put their terrible past behind them and carve out a better future for their nation? They will have to rise above their divisions to do so.

Land and Climate

The sharp divisions among Iraq's people are reflected in its landscape. Iraq is a country of harsh extremes—heat and cold, drought and rain, plains and mountains. But even though survival in Iraq is hard, people have lived there throughout human history.

Iraq is 167,975 square miles in area, slightly larger than twice the size of Idaho.[1] It is bordered

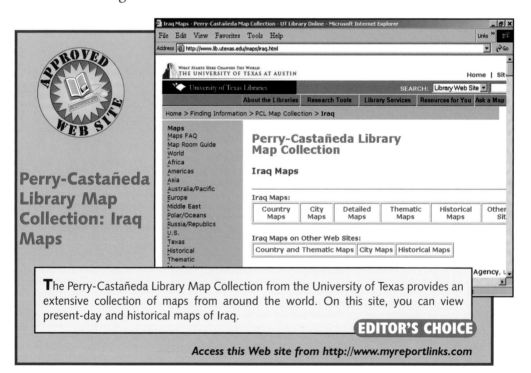

Perry-Castañeda Library Map Collection: Iraq Maps

The Perry-Castañeda Library Map Collection from the University of Texas provides an extensive collection of maps from around the world. On this site, you can view present-day and historical maps of Iraq.

EDITOR'S CHOICE

Access this Web site from http://www.myreportlinks.com

by Turkey, Iran, Kuwait, Saudi Arabia, Jordan, and Syria. Iraq is the most landlocked Middle Eastern country after Jordan. In the southeast, a 36-mile strip of coastline along the Persian Gulf is the country's only access to the sea.[2] Among Iraq's most famous geographical features are the Tigris and Euphrates rivers and its oil fields. The rivers symbolize the country's distant past, the oil fields its troubled present.

Rivers and Oil Fields

The Tigris and Euphrates rivers originate in Turkey, pass through Syria, and make the longest part of their journey through Iraq. The fertile farmland around the southern part of these rivers is known as the Cradle of Civilization. This is because the area was the home of the world's earliest known civilization some five thousand years ago. Iraq also contains the largest part of a broad region known as the Fertile Crescent, where the fertile soil allowed many civilizations to develop in ancient times.

By contrast, the country's oil fields represent modern Iraq. Throughout much of the last hundred years, Iraq's rich reserves of oil have played a key role in Iraqi history. In so harsh a country, oil production alone keeps Iraq's people out of serious poverty. It has also had a great affect on Iraq's international relations.

Iraq is often divided into four regions: deserts, highlands, rolling uplands, and alluvial plains (regions smoothed and leveled by streams and flooding).

Desert

About two fifths of Iraq is desert, stretching through the west and southwest. Parts of this desert are rocky, rugged, and barren, while other parts are sandy and scrubby. Almost the only people who live in Iraq's deserts are Bedouins. These are nomadic, animal-herding Arab people who have learned to live in the Middle East's harshest areas.

Iraq's barren desert area leaves the country open to attack, as the coalition invasion of 2003 proved. Thousands of armored vehicles stormed through the desert on their way to Iraq's capital of Baghdad. This activity disturbed the desert's ecology. The desert soil is normally protected by a thin layer of pebbles, many of which were thrown aside by vehicles, sending dust into the air. Much of this dust remained airborne, causing health and visibility hazards. Loose soil also created sand dunes, which harmed roads, airport runways, and Bedouin homes.[3]

Northeastern Highlands

The northeastern part of Iraq is a highland region. It is inhabited largely by the Kurds, a fiercely

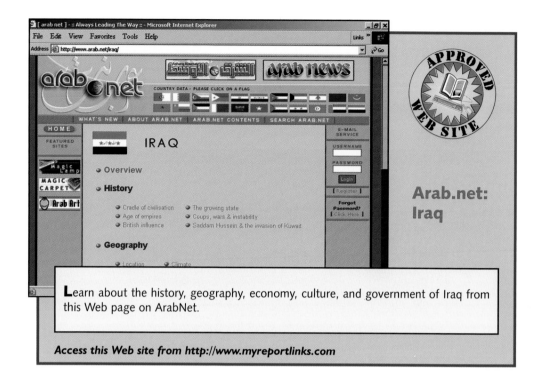

Learn about the history, geography, economy, culture, and government of Iraq from this Web page on ArabNet.

Access this Web site from http://www.myreportlinks.com

independent ethnic group that has often been at odds with Iraq's past governments.

Iraq's highlands share the Zagros Mountains with neighboring Iran. These mountains are the only places in Iraq where forests can be found. Among the Zagros Mountains is one of Iraq's highest peaks, Haji Ibrahim. This mountain, which stands at the border with Iran, is 11,811 feet high.

Much of the rest of the highland region consists of hills, foothills, and steppes. Such high country contrasts sharply with other parts of Iraq, where the land seldom rises above a thousand feet.

The highlands also feature a much different climate than other parts of Iraq. Snow often falls

▲ *This United States soldier is positioned in a hilly region of northern Iraq.*

there during the cold winters. Rains fall upon the highlands from October to May—the only significant rainfall in the country. Rain makes planting possible in the lower steppes and foothills, so about half of Iraq's farmable land can be found in the highlands. The rest of this hilly, rocky region is suitable only for grazing livestock.

With a population of about 710,000, the most important city in this region is Kirkuk. It is one of Iraq's most important oil-producing centers.

▷ Rolling Uplands

Between the Tigris and Euphrates rivers in northern Iraq lies a region that is mostly a plateau. It is called Al Jazirah, an Arabic word meaning "the island." This region includes the Sinjar Mountains, which only reach a height of 4,448 feet—much lower than the Zagros Mountains to the east. The Sinjar Mountains are home to a small religious sect called the Yezidis.

Al Jazirah's main waterway is a stream called Wadi Tharthar. Other streams cut through this region's valleys. Even so, Al Jazirah is considered a desert because it receives too little rain for planting, and water cannot be brought to the area artificially. Also, there are several salt flats in the region where farming or grazing is impossible.

At the eastern edge of Al Jazirah is the city of Mosul, Iraq's second largest city. Like Kirkuk, Mosul is a major petroleum center.

▶ Alluvial Plains

Iraq's alluvial plains include the richest farmland in southwest Asia. This is why civilization started there, and why the region is the most populous part of Iraq today. The plains begin north of the city of Baghdad and continue south to the Persian Gulf. Rich soil is deposited through this region by the Tigris and Euphrates rivers.

Despite the richness of the soil, farming on the alluvial plains has never been easy. Much of the land between the Tigris and Euphrates lies below the levels of the rivers themselves. As a result, the region suffered from unpredictable flooding for thousands of years.

Climate is another problem. Although winter temperatures are cool, the weather can be extremely hot during the long summers. July and August temperatures in Baghdad are often around 92°F, and they have been known to reach as high as 123°F. In the marshy, southernmost parts of this region, some of the highest temperatures in the world have been recorded. Humidity is also extremely high there.

Perhaps worst of all, little rain falls upon the alluvial plains—only about six inches a year. The solution to this problem has always been irrigation—artificially channeling water from rivers and lakes to farmlands. The first irrigation in Iraq was practiced between 5600 and 5000 B.C. by a prehistoric culture now called the Samarra.[4] Iraqis have irrigated the alluvial plains ever since.

▶ Water Systems

People have been building other water systems in Iraq for thousands of years. For example, the Shatt-el-Hai Canal was built around 2200 B.C., connecting the Tigris and Euphrates rivers.[5] During the twentieth century, efforts to control water were vastly increased. Dams have been built, canals expanded, and irrigation systems improved.

▲ *The Marsh Arabs have lived in the marshlands between the Euphrates and Tigris rivers since ancient times.*

Despite the help of irrigation and flood control, Iraqi agriculture is limited by ecological problems. Even irrigation causes damage, because it slowly deposits salt from the water into the farmland. As a result, the alluvial plains are far less rich for farming now than they were in ancient times.[6]

Some of Saddam Hussein's other water control efforts caused ecological harm—at times deliberately. In the southeast part of Iraq, the Tigris and Euphrates rivers join to form the Shatt al Arab River, which flows into the Persian Gulf. About 5,600 square miles of marshlands once surrounded the area of the Shatt al Arab.[7] In 1991, Hussein ordered the construction of dikes and channels to drain these marshes—officially for "security reasons."[8]

These marshlands were the home to Marsh Arabs, who resisted Hussein's regime. Hussein set about destroying their environment in order to punish them. By 2002, the marshlands had shrunk to about 470 square miles.[9] Some seventy thousand marsh dwellers were forced to flee to camps in neighboring Iran.

However, this situation is beginning to improve. Immediately after Hussein was removed from power, local people began to destroy the dikes that had drained the marshes. As a result, reports in 2005 showed that over 37 percent of the marshlands had returned. Whether the marshes will ever be fully restored to their original state remains to be seen.

Iraq's largest oil fields lie in the southeast. Many of these are near the city of Basra, which leads even Kirkuk and Mosul as the country's most important petroleum center.

▶ Wildlife

Despite Iraq's harsh environment, a broad variety of animals live throughout the country. Wildlife includes antelope, gazelles, bats, hares, cheetahs, wild pigs, hyenas, jackals, and various kinds of lizards. The lion is extinct in Iraq, and the ostrich and wild ass are nearly so.

▲ *Gazelles are one of the many interesting animals native to Iraq.*

Ecological problems, especially the draining of southern marshes, have disturbed bird migration patterns. Even so, there remain many kinds of birds in Iraq. Birds of prey include owls, hawks, buzzards, ravens, and vultures. Other birds include geese, sand grouse, ducks, and partridge.

Religion

The vast majority of Iraqis, about 97 percent of them, are Muslims.[1] Among Iraq's smaller religious groups are Christians, Yezidis, Mandeans, and Sufis. For centuries, a small but significant number of Jews inhabited what is now Iraq, living peacefully with the Muslim majority. But during the early 1940s, Iraqi Jews became victims of persecution and violence, and most fled the country.[2]

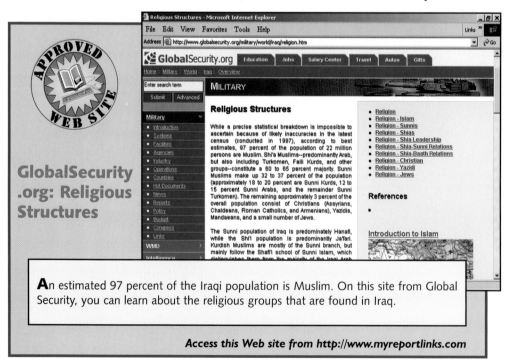

GlobalSecurity .org: Religious Structures

An estimated 97 percent of the Iraqi population is Muslim. On this site from Global Security, you can learn about the religious groups that are found in Iraq.

Access this Web site from http://www.myreportlinks.com

Today, only about twenty-five hundred Jews live in Iraq, all of them in Baghdad.[3]

One would think that widespread Iraqi devotion to Islam would contribute to national unity. However, Iraqi Muslims are deeply divided between Sunni and Shi'a, the two main branches of Islam. Other Islamic nations are dominated by one of these branches or the other. For example, the great majority of Iranians are Shi'ites, while the great majority of Saudi Arabians are Sunnis.

But the Sunnis and Shi'ites are more evenly balanced in Iraq than in any other Islamic country, although there is a Shi'a majority. Sunnis are primarily centered in the middle of the country, around Baghdad, while Shi'ites are primarily centered in the south, around Basra. Conflict between these groups has caused much of Iraq's violence and political divisions that followed the fall of Hussein. To understand how this came about, it is necessary to take a quick look at the history of Islam itself.

▶ The Founding of Islam

The religion of Islam was founded by the Prophet Muhammad, who was born in the city of Mecca (now in Saudi Arabia) in A.D. 570. Although he was orphaned and suffered from poverty as a child, he became a wealthy merchant during his early adulthood.

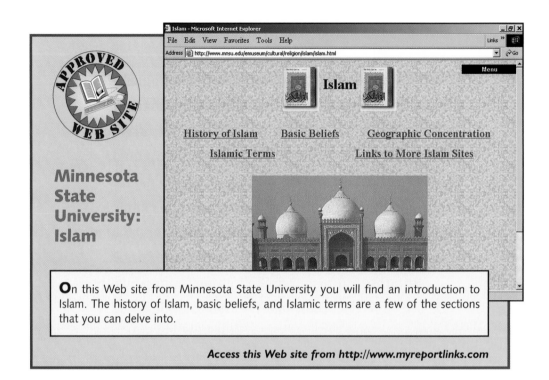

Islam - Microsoft Internet Explorer

File   Edit   View   Favorites   Tools   Help

Address http://www.mnsu.edu/emuseum/cultural/religion/islam/islam.html

Menu

Islam

History of Islam   Basic Beliefs   Geographic Concentration

Islamic Terms   Links to More Islam Sites

Minnesota State University: Islam

On this Web site from Minnesota State University you will find an introduction to Islam. The history of Islam, basic beliefs, and Islamic terms are a few of the sections that you can delve into.

Access this Web site from http://www.myreportlinks.com

In those days, the Arabian people were poly-theistic—that is, they believed in more than one god. It has been said that some 360 gods and goddesses were worshipped in Arabia during Muhammad's early years.[4] According to Islamic belief, even as a boy, Muhammad had a strong dislike for polytheism.

When he was forty years old, Muhammad began to receive what Muslims believe to have been revelations (religious messages) from the angel Gabriel. These revelations were eventually collected in the Qur'an, Islam's most sacred book. Muhammad believed that he was the last in a line of prophets that included Adam, Noah, Abraham, Moses, and Jesus.

Muhammad called upon Arabs to worship Allah, the Arabic name for the Jewish and Christian God. Muhammad's message of monotheism (belief in a single god) was received with hostility at first. In 622, he and his followers were forced to flee Mecca, which they considered to be a holy city. They went north to live in Medina (also now in Saudi Arabia).

Muhammad's followers in Medina and the Meccans who worshipped multiple gods warred for several years. Muhammad's forces were eventually victorious, seizing Mecca without a fight in 630. Soon, almost all of Arabia became part of an Islamic state. By the time of his death in 632, Muhammad was the region's most powerful religious and political leader, with about one hundred thousand followers.[5] Within a century after his death, the Islamic empire had spread westward across Africa to southern Spain, and westward across Asia to India. Islam eventually reached as far east as China, Indonesia, and the Malay Peninsula.

The Division of Islam

For centuries after Muhammad's death, the Islamic world was ruled by leaders called caliphs.

The tomb of Ali is located in Najaf, Iraq. It is a very holy site for Shi'a Muslims.

The choice of the first caliph began more than a thousand years of controversy.

After Muhammad died, a group of Muslims, who later called themselves Sunnis, elected Muhammad's comrade Abu Bakr the first caliph. A smaller group of Muslims, who later called themselves Shi'ites, or the Shi'a, considered this a mistake. They felt that Muhammad's son-in-law, Ali, should have been the first caliph.

Ali did, in fact, become the fourth caliph in 656. After Ali's death, Shi'ites insisted that only Muhammad's direct descendants should be caliphs. By contrast, Sunnis felt that any elected caliphs were legitimate.[6] The controversy continues today, even though nobody has held the title of caliph since 1924.

Differences Small and Large

Shi'ites and Sunnis alike consider themselves to be devout Muslims and share most of the same beliefs and practices. Even so, differences have grown between them over the centuries. To non-Muslims, some of these differences may seem fairly trivial. For example, Sunnis lower their heads onto mats in prayer, while Shi'ites lower their heads onto pieces of hard clay.

But other differences are more profound. Some have to do with the nature of Allah and human will. Sunnis believe that Allah has a body with humanlike limbs and that Allah can sometimes be seen. Shi'ites believe that Allah has no body and can never be seen. Moreover, Sunnis believe that Allah dictates all human actions. By contrast, Shi'ites believe that Allah knows in advance of all human acts but does not make people do them.[7]

Shi'ites and Sunnis in Iraqi Politics

While Shi'ites make up only about 10 to 15 percent of Muslims worldwide, in Iraq they are the majority. About 32 to 37 percent of Iraq's population is Sunni; about 60 to 65 percent Shi'ite.[8] Even so, the country's Sunni long held power over the Shi'a.

Sunni power in Iraq dates back to the Turkish Ottoman Empire. This empire reached its height during the fifteenth and sixteenth centuries, ruling the entire Arabian world. In those days, the nation of Iraq did not yet exist. The region consisted instead of the provinces of Mosul, Baghdad, and Basra. Because the Shi'ites of the region disliked Ottoman rule, the empire placed local power into the hands of Sunnis.[9]

The Ottoman Empire collapsed after World War I (1914–18). The British then took control of the region that included Mosul, Baghdad, and Basra and named it Iraq. The British continued to allow Sunnis to exercise local power there, despite the fact that there were many more Shi'as.[10] Sunni political dominance did not wane

▲ *These Iraqis are hanging out in front of the Walls of Nineveh in Mosul. When Britain transferred power to an Iraqi government, it left Sunni Muslims in charge of Mosul and the surrounding area.*

after Iraq achieved its independence in 1932. It continued through the regime of Saddam Hussein, who is a Sunni.

The 2003 invasion of Iraq ended centuries of Sunni political rule. Moreover, the Sunni minority will surely not rule again under a democratic government. This change in their status has alarmed many Sunnis, who fear a transition of power to the Shi'a. Such fears caused some Sunni religious leaders to call for a boycott of the January 2005 elections. It remains uncertain whether a democratic constitution can survive Sunni political resistance.

Radical Sunnis have also played a leading part in the insurgency, which is increasingly directed against Shi'ites. International observers worry that conflict between Sunnis and Shi'ites will erupt into civil war. Some believe that a civil war is already underway.

Church and State

Conflict between Sunnis and Shi'ites is not the only problem presented by religion in Iraq. The role of Islam in the nation's future government is also a serious issue.

According to the laws of Western democracies, church and state should be kept separate in a free society. For this reason, the First Amendment of the

This up-to-date Web site from the Bureau of Near Eastern Affairs contains a variety of information about Iraq's neighbor, Iran.

Access this Web site from http://www.myreportlinks.com

U.S. Constitution's Bill of Rights forbids passing any law "respecting an establishment of religion, or prohibiting the free exercise thereof. . . ." By contrast, it is widely believed throughout the Islamic world that nations must be governed by sharia (Islamic law).

Even so, separation of church and state existed in Iraq before the coalition invasion. From 1968 until 2003, Iraq was ruled by the Ba'ath party, which Saddam Hussein led after 1978. Unlike most governments throughout the Islamic world, Iraq's Ba'ath government was secular (not ruled by religious law).

Iraqi Muslims, whether Shi'ite or Sunni, are deeply religious people. Now that they are free from Hussein's tyranny, some question whether they will continue to practice separation of church and state. The United States is especially concerned that Iraq will become an Islamic theocracy (government based on divine law) like Iran, which is deeply hostile to the West.

▷ New Constitution

The newest attempt at an Iraqi constitution raises concerns about this issue. On one hand, the constitution forbids passing any laws that contradict the principles of democracy. It also vows to protect basic human rights and freedoms. On the other hand, the constitutional draft forbids passing any law "that contradicts the undisputed rules of Islam."[11] The inclusion of this phrase troubles many people, especially women's rights advocates.

Women and Islam

Some Islamic countries have women's rights records that are suspect. In Saudi Arabia, for example, women are not allowed to have driver's licenses and must cover their faces in public.[12] Under Afghanistan's oppressive Taliban regime (1996–2001), women were not permitted to leave their houses unless accompanied by male family members.[13] According to fundamentalist Muslims, these and even harsher restrictions are part of Islamic law.

Saddam Hussein's regime was brutal to both women and men. But even under his reign, women enjoyed more rights than did women of neighboring Islamic nations. In 1970, the secular Ba'ath party declared men and women to be equals. Women were allowed to work freely, earn equal pay as men, serve in the armed forces, and dress as they liked. Miniskirts were not uncommon during the 1970s and 1980s—an unthinkable sight in today's Saudi Arabia or Iran.

In 1980, Hussein granted women the right to vote. Although elections under his regime were fixed, and therefore meaningless, women did

Women in Iraq steadily lost some of their rights during the 1990s and the last years of Saddam Hussein's rule. It remains to be seen which rights they will have under the next Iraqi constitution.

assume many prominent political positions under his rule.

Women's rights deteriorated during the 1990s. During that decade of war and economic hardship, Hussein found it increasingly necessary to please fundamentalist Muslims. He permitted polygamy (letting a man have more than one wife) and segregated schools according to gender. More alarmingly, he legalized "honor killings," in which male family members murder girls and women suspected of sexual misconduct.[14]

Even so, women still had important rights at the end of Hussein's regime. Today, many Iraqi women are determined to keep their freedoms. They are encouraged that the constitution asserts the equality of Iraqi men and women. But whether women's rights will prevail if religion plays an increasing role in Iraqi government remains to be seen.

Iraqi Culture

It is unfortunate that most Westerners do not feel safe traveling to Iraq these days. If they could, they would see a land where civilized culture has existed for five thousand years. Between ten thousand and one hundred thousand Iraqi archeological sites show how human history itself got started.[1]

A form of writing called cuneiform was invented in ancient Mesopotamia. This cuneiform wedge was carved around 3100 B.C. Browse this, and other images of Mesopotamia, at the **Wars and Conflict: Iraq: Conflict in Context** Web page.

Iraq's ruins include the four-thousand-year-old ziggurat (temple tower) of Ur, an architectural wonder that rivals works of the later Egyptians and Greeks.

The National Museum of Iraq in Baghdad is an amazing storehouse of antiquity. It features cups, vases, jewelry, sculptures, and many other precious artifacts dating to the dawn of civilization. It also includes many clay tablets inscribed with cuneiform, one of the world's earliest forms of writing.

▷ Historical Riches

Among these writings is the Code of Hammurabi, a collection of laws dating to about 1700 B.C. Also included is *The Epic of Gilgamesh,* a world masterpiece completed in the seventh century B.C. In the words of historian Georges Roux: "[T]here are few countries in the world where the past is more strangely alive, where the historian's dead texts are provided with a more appropriate illustration."[2]

Sadly, the violence of recent years has harmed Iraq's historical riches. Many of Iraq's archeological sites—including the ziggurat at Ur—have been damaged by bombing and looting.[3] After the fall of Baghdad in April 2003, looters stormed the National Museum, destroying much of what they found inside. Looters stole some fifteen thousand precious objects. As of October 2004, only about

Two Yezidis in front of a shrine in Sheikh Adi, Iraq.

three thousand of these priceless objects had been recovered. The quest to restore Iraq's ancient treasures will doubtless continue for years.[4]

Today's Iraqis

Since ancient times, many different peoples have populated the region now known as Iraq. Today, Arabs are Iraq's largest ethnic group, while Kurds are the second largest. There are several smaller ethnic groups.

Turkomans, who make up less than 2 percent of Iraq's population, live between the Kurdish and Arabic regions of Iraq. They are descended from the Turkish people, speak a Turkish dialect, and sometimes find themselves in conflict with their neighboring Kurds. Most Turkomans belong to the Sunni branch of Islam.

Numbering about 133,000 people, Iraq's Assyrians make up less than one percent of Iraq's population. They are descended from the ancient Mesopotamians, who created the world's first civilizations in the region. Today, Assyrians live primarily in cities, practice several forms of Christianity, and speak a language called Aramaic.

Descendant from Kurds, but separate from today's Kurds are Iraq's Yezidis. This group is marked by unusual religious beliefs. Their faith blends Christianity, Islam, Judaism, and other religions. They worship an angel named Malak Taus, whom they believe fell from grace from heaven and was later restored to glory.[5] There are perhaps five hundred thousand Yezidis in the world. Iraqi Yezidis live mostly in the Sinjar Mountains and speak a Kurdish dialect.

There are other small ethnic groups in Iraq. These include an ancient people called Armenians, desert-dwelling Bedouins, and the Lur, who speak Farsi and live near the border of Iran.

The Kadhimain shrine in Baghdad, Iraq's capital and largest city.

Arabs

Arabs make up 75 to 80 percent of the Iraqi people.[6] Arabs worldwide number about 250 million and live mostly in North Africa and the Middle East. Their original homeland, Hijaz, is now part of Saudi Arabia. It was in Hijaz that Muhammad converted the Arabic people to Islam. The majority of Arabs remain Muslims today.

Typically, Arabs are dark-haired, brown-eyed, and somewhat light-skinned. The Arabic people, though, are of a wide mix of races, so their appearances can range from very dark to very light.[7] In fact, Arabic identity has little to do with race or ancestry. People identify themselves as Arabs for several reasons—for example, if they live in an Arabic nation, follow Arabic customs, or speak Arabic.

Except in the northeastern part of Iraq, where most of the nation's Kurds live, Arabs dominate almost all aspects of Iraqi life, including its politics.

Kurds

Kurds make up 15 to 20 percent of Iraq's population, most of them living in the northeast part of the country.[8] These people inhabit a region called Kurdistan, which includes parts of Turkey, Syria, Iraq, Iran, Azerbaijan, and Armenia. There are between 15 and 25 million Kurds today, most of them living in Turkey.

▲ An image of a Kurd woman and her children sitting in a field. The image was taken between 1905 and 1915.

After World War I, the Middle East was carved into nation-states that included Iraq. The Kurds were promised a nation of their own, but this promise was not kept. Ever since then, Kurds throughout Kurdistan have struggled for independence. Iraqi Kurds are no exception. Generally, they do not really consider themselves Iraqi, and have often rebelled against Iraqi rule.

Saddam Hussein was particularly harsh in putting down Kurdish rebellions. In 1987–88, he used chemical weapons against the Kurds.[9] But after Hussein's defeat in the first Persian Gulf War of 1991, the United Nations (UN) took steps to protect the Kurds. The UN established a safe haven for them above the 36th parallel (line of latitude). Since then, Iraqi Kurds have been somewhat autonomous (politically independent).

Kurds were once a mainly rural people who herded sheep and goats and lived a nomadic lifestyle (moving frequently from place to place). But today, the majority of Kurds live on farms, in villages, or in cities. Most belong to the Sunni branch of Islam.

▷ Families and Tribes

Iraqi families tend to be patriarchal (dominated by males). The oldest male typically makes all the major family decisions, ranging from marriage to business. Male children often have more advantages and opportunities than female children. This is especially true when it comes to employment. They also inherit more of the family's wealth. By contrast, women have few family rights. Even if they work outside the home, they are expected to tend to domestic duties and raise children.

In Iraq, extended families (families that include a range of relatives) are more common than nuclear families (families that consist of a mother, a father, and their children). In rural parts of Iraq, several generations of a family often live in a single household.

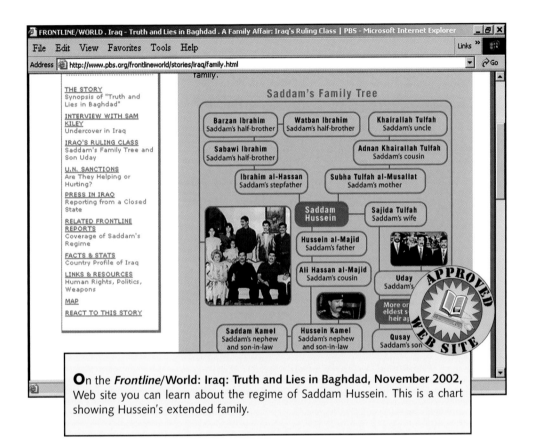

FRONTLINE/WORLD . Iraq - Truth and Lies in Baghdad . A Family Affair: Iraq's Ruling Class | PBS - Microsoft Internet Explorer

File   Edit   View   Favorites   Tools   Help   Links »

Address http://www.pbs.org/frontlineworld/stories/iraq/family.html

THE STORY
Synopsis of "Truth and
Lies in Baghdad"

INTERVIEW WITH SAM
KILEY
Undercover in Iraq

IRAQ'S RULING CLASS
Saddam's Family Tree and
Son Uday

U.N. SANCTIONS
Are They Helping or
Hurting?

PRESS IN IRAQ
Reporting from a Closed
State

RELATED FRONTLINE
REPORTS
Coverage of Saddam's
Regime

FACTS & STATS
Country Profile of Iraq

LINKS & RESOURCES
Human Rights, Politics,
Weapons

MAP

REACT TO THIS STORY

Saddam's Family Tree

Barzan Ibrahim
Saddam's half-brother

Watban Ibrahim
Saddam's half-brother

Khairallah Tulfah
Saddam's uncle

Sabawi Ibrahim
Saddam's half-brother

Adnan Khairallah Tulfah
Saddam's cousin

Ibrahim al-Hassan
Saddam's stepfather

Subha Tulfah al-Musallat
Saddam's mother

Saddam Hussein

Sajida Tulfah
Saddam's wife

Hussein al-Majid
Saddam's father

Ali Hassan al-Majid
Saddam's cousin

Uday
Saddam's

More or
eldest s
heir ap

Saddam Kamel
Saddam's nephew
and son-in-law

Hussein Kamel
Saddam's nephew
and son-in-law

Qusay
Saddam's son

On the *Frontline*/World: Iraq: Truth and Lies in Baghdad, November 2002, Web site you can learn about the regime of Saddam Hussein. This is a chart showing Hussein's extended family.

The extended family is called the *khams*. A group of such families is called a house, or *beit*. A still larger unit built upon beits is the clan, or *fakhdh*. A group of fakhdhs make up a tribe, led by a chieftain called a *shaikh*. There are about 150 tribes in Iraq, which are organized into federations of tribes, or *qabila*.

Family and tribal connections are profoundly important to most Iraqis. In fact, nearly half of Iraqis feel deeper loyalty to their tribes and families than they do to the nation itself. This situation has long created difficulties in maintaining a strong central government.

Since tribes can include many thousands of members, they exercise great influence on Iraqi politics. Saddam Hussein, for example, came from the al-Bu Nasir tribe of Tikrit. Hussein took care to grant political power to family members and others in the al-Bu Nasir. This tactic helped Hussein maintain his own dictatorial powers.[10]

Languages

The Kurds of northern Iraq speak Kurdish, which is related to the Farsi language spoken in neighboring Iran. Throughout the rest of Iraq, Arabic is the most widely spoken language.

There are three basic forms of Arabic. Classical Arabic is the language of the Qur'an and other writings of early Islam. It is rarely spoken nowadays except by Bedouins. Modern Standard Arabic is the literary form of the language. It is considered proper Arabic, even though many Arabs cannot speak it fluently. Spoken Arabic, though less formal, is the language actually used by most Arabs.

Iraqis speak several different dialects (local varieties) of Arabic. Other languages spoken in Iraq include Assyrian, Armenian, Chaldean, Syriac, Turkish, and Farsi. All these dialects and languages sometimes make it difficult for Iraqis to understand one another. Fortunately, many Iraqis are bilingual (able to speak two languages).

English is the most widely spoken foreign language in Iraq. It is taught in schools and often used in business matters.[11]

▶ Rural and City Life

Iraqis living a rural lifestyle are found mainly in two regions—the Kurdish highlands in the northeast, and the alluvial plains in the southeast. Rural Kurds tend to live in small, isolated farms and villages and raise livestock. Southern Iraqis use irrigation to practice farming, much as people have done for thousands of years. Villages in the alluvial plains typically have between one hundred and two thousand houses.

Iraqi rural life is declining despite government efforts to promote farming and villages. More than three fifths of Iraqis now live in urban areas, especially large cities like Baghdad, Mosul, and Basra.

Founded in A.D. 762, Baghdad lies near the center of Iraq, with a population of about 7.4 million people. The city is Iraq's leading cultural, political, and economic center. Moreover, despite damage to the city from recent wars, it offers more public services than other Iraqi cities. So people continue to migrate to Baghdad, fleeing poor conditions elsewhere. Perhaps as much as one third of the country's population now lives in Baghdad.

Iraq's second largest city, Mosul, lies in the northwest part of the country on the Tigris River.

▲ *Baghdad is the leading cultural center of Iraq. This is the square in front of the Kahimain shrine.*

With about 1.3 million inhabitants, it is populated mainly by Kurds, with Assyrian and Turkoman minorities. It is an important oil-producing center.

Iraq's third largest city is Basra, which lies south of Baghdad along the Shatt al Arab River. It was once Iraq's second largest city. But Basra's infrastructure (public necessities including roads, schools, hospitals, power, water, police, etc.) was badly damaged by the Persian Gulf War of 1991. As a result, many people left Basra to live in Baghdad. Now the city has a population of only about 990,000. It has also been replaced by its neighboring city of Umm Qasr as Iraq's key shipping port. However, Basra still remains Iraq's most important oil-producing center.[12]

Social Customs

Iraqi men and women typically behave quite differently in public. Male friends kiss and hold hands upon greeting one another. Women are not so openly affectionate, especially with men. When meeting a man in public, a woman merely says, "Salaam Alaykom" ("Peace be with you"). Moreover, men and women simply do not have casual friendships with one another outside of the family.

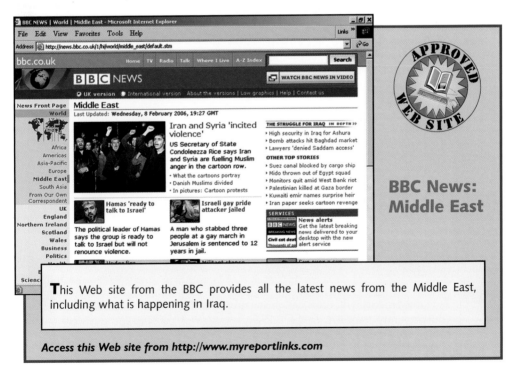

BBC News: Middle East

This Web site from the BBC provides all the latest news from the Middle East, including what is happening in Iraq.

Access this Web site from http://www.myreportlinks.com

Iraqis value politeness. It is considered poor manners to point one's finger while talking, or to gesture with the left hand. And when handing something to another person, one should always do it with the right hand or with both hands. Men must even be careful how they sit. Crossing one's legs is thought to be rude, so is allowing the sole of the foot to face someone.

Hospitality, too, is marked by elaborate manners and customs. Houseguests remove their shoes at the door upon arriving, then usually wear slippers offered by the host. After the host shows

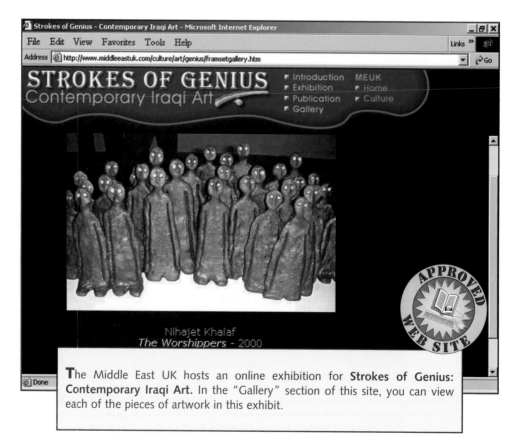

The Middle East UK hosts an online exhibition for **Strokes of Genius: Contemporary Iraqi Art.** In the "Gallery" section of this site, you can view each of the pieces of artwork in this exhibit.

guests inside, everyone sits on cushions or on the floor. If a guest offers the host a gift, the host is likely to refuse it politely several times before accepting it.[13]

Iraqis are not as concerned as Westerners about scheduling visits. Typically, an Iraqi home is always open to friends and relatives.

The Arts

Because the state of Iraq was artificially created after World War I, Iraqis have long struggled to create a national identity. For almost a century, artists and writers have played an important role in this process. During the 1920s, poets such as Ahmad al-Safi al-Najafi, Ma'ruf al-Rusafi, and Muhammad Mahdi al-Jawahiri offered visions of what it meant to be Iraqi. They also protested foreign occupation and economic injustice within the country.[14]

Today's Iraqi artists continue this effort to forge a sense of national self. In addition to expressing an Arabic and Islamic sensibility, their works often refer to Iraq's ancient civilizations.

Several recent exhibitions have introduced Westerners to contemporary Iraqi art. Late in 2000, London's Brunei Gallery featured an exhibition called *Strokes of Genius: Contemporary Iraqi Art*. This exhibition toured Great Britain in 2001 and America in 2002. It emphasized the works of younger Iraqi artists, many of whom were forced into exile during Saddam Hussein's dictatorship. In January 2002, Grinnell College in Iowa also sponsored a series of events featuring Iraqi artists in exile. These events ranged from poetry readings to exhibitions.

While many artists went into exile during Hussein's regime, others continued to work in Iraq. Iraq's performing arts—ballet, theater, and music—thrived even under the dictatorship. Censorship was, of course, a problem. Moreover, Iraqi visual artists were forced to create countless images glorifying Hussein.

How will the arts in Iraq fare now that Hussein has fallen? Not all signs are encouraging. Some Iraqi artists feel as reluctant to express themselves freely under the United States-led occupation as they did under Hussein's regime. They also worry about who will come to power after the occupation ends.[15] The future of artistic expression in Iraq is as uncertain as the nation's destiny.

▶ Education

For many years, Iraq's educational system was a source of national pride. The country used to produce a large number of scientists, administrators, technicians, and skilled workers. Even today, the government continues to fund schooling at all levels. Primary education is required.

▲ Although many parts of Iraq have been ravaged by war, Iraqis are still trying to put an emphasis on education. In this photo, U.S. Army Captain Sam Donnelly hands out diplomas to students at a graduation ceremony in Tikrit, Iraq.

The years between 1976 and 1986 brought spectacular growth to Iraq's schools. The number of students pursuing higher education increased rapidly. Moreover, the opportunity for Iraqi women to learn was remarkable by Middle East standards. By 1986, 44 percent of Iraq's primary-school students were females, as were 55 percent of its secondary-school students.[16] At times, more women than men graduated from universities.

However, Iraq's educational system suffered during many long years of war, beginning with the Iran-Iraq War (1980–88). The Ba'ath regime struggled to keep educational excellence alive. For example, college students were not drafted into military service.[17]

Iraqi education declined nonetheless. During the economic hardships of the 1990s, many students had to leave school to work. Moreover, Iraq's growing isolation from much of the world lowered the quality of teaching materials. Iraq's schools gradually became poorer than those of other Middle-Eastern countries. Rebuilding a once-excellent school system is now a huge task for the Iraqi people.

The Media

Under Hussein's dictatorship, most media were owned and controlled by the government. Iraqi media included a national television service, local

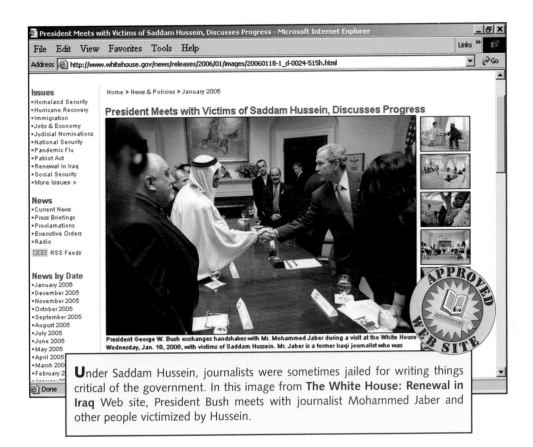

President Meets with Victims of Saddam Hussein, Discusses Progress - Microsoft Internet Explorer

Under Saddam Hussein, journalists were sometimes jailed for writing things critical of the government. In this image from **The White House: Renewal in Iraq** Web site, President Bush meets with journalist Mohammed Jaber and other people victimized by Hussein.

television stations, and six Arabic newspapers. Not surprisingly, the public received a limited range of viewpoints.

After Hussein's downfall in 2003, Iraq experienced an explosion of media. A couple of months after the invasion, the number of newspapers in Baghdad alone rose to sixty.[18] The number of newspapers nationwide reached two hundred by March 2004.[19] Few observers doubt that Iraq now enjoys much greater freedom of press than most

Arabic countries. The quality of Iraqi journalism, however, is another issue.

In June 2003, the Arab Press Freedom Watch criticized Iraqi news media. It determined that only three of the huge number of Iraqi newspapers showed reasonable quality. Others were mostly owned by political parties or influential political figures. This situation resulted in the publication of wider-ranging views, but not independent and reliable information.

The Arab Freedom Watch also observed that a lack of training among journalists was a great problem. After so many years of state censorship and control, journalists simply did not know their craft. Even their Arabic grammar was faulty.[20] The London-based Institute of War and Peace Reporting came to similar conclusions in 2004.[21]

The improvement of Iraqi media will depend on many factors. Independent control of news outlets would help. As would better journalistic training. Efforts are being made in this direction. In August 2005, six Iraqi journalists created a group called the Afaq Media Forum. Its purpose is to promote better quality journalism in Iraq.[22]

▶ Sports

Soccer is the most popular sport in Iraq. Huge crowds watch soccer games in Baghdad's Al-Sha'b Stadium, and many more watch Iraqis play on television. However, during the reign of Saddam Hussein, soccer was a dangerous game to play.

Uday Hussein, Saddam's son, personally took charge of Iraq's participation in international athletic events. A vicious man, Uday tortured athletes who failed to live up to his expectations. He was especially brutal toward soccer players. Failure to win a tournament might mean having one's legs beaten with a cane or being forced to kick concrete balls.[23] Players who failed to score goals, or failed to prevent rivals from scoring, were often imprisoned. Their warders shaved their heads to mark them as failures.[24]

Uday Hussein was in charge of the Iraqi National Olympic Committee from 1984 until Iraq was invaded by coalition forces in 2003. During his time as head of the committee, he was accused of torture and harsh punishments. This article from ESPN examines the dark period of his leadership.

Access this Web site from http://www.myreportlinks.com

Uday's tactics did nothing to improve the performance of Iraqi athletes. For many years, the nation's soccer team failed to qualify for the Olympics. The only Olympic medal ever won by an Iraqi athlete was a bronze (third place) medal for weightlifting in 1960. That was long before Hussein came to power.

After the fall of Hussein and the killing of Uday by United States forces, Iraqi soccer players could play without fear. Iraq's team qualified for the 2004 Summer Olympics and competed in Greece. Iraq had an impressive run of victories, but ended up finishing fourth. Even without a medal, the nation's pride in its soccer athletes had at last been restored.

Religious Holy Days and Observances

Because Muslims make up the majority in Iraq, Islamic holy days are carefully observed. From a Western perspective, the dates for these days are constantly shifting. This is because Muslims follow a lunar calendar instead of a solar calendar. Consequently, the Islamic year is somewhat shorter than a Western year.

Early in the year is the Hajj—the annual pilgrimage to Mecca. Every Muslim is required to make this pilgrimage at least once in a lifetime if at all possible. More than 2 million Muslims join in this pilgrimage every year.

▲ *Muslims pray five times a day facing the direction of the city of Mecca, Saudi Arabia.*

Muslims also observe Ramadan. This is a month of dawn-to-sunset fasting in search of self-purification and moral excellence. It is celebrated in the ninth month of the lunar calendar. This means that it always falls about thirteen days before the previous year. Ramadan is followed by Eid ul-Fitr, a three-day celebration and feast that breaks the fast.

Muslims must actively practice their faith every day, not just on special occasions. They are required to pray five times daily—in the morning, after midday, between midday and sunset, right after sunset, and an hour after sunset. Each prayer must be made facing the city of Mecca.

Iraqi Cuisine

Iraqis are proud of their cuisine, which they regard as the greatest in the world. When Arabs arrived in what is now Iraq and took over the region, the food there took on a markedly Arabic character. Countless other cultures and civilizations have influenced Iraqi cuisine, which today also resembles that of Greece, Turkey, and Iran.[25]

Common staples in Iraqi food are rice, unleavened bread, spiced meat, and stuffed vegetables.

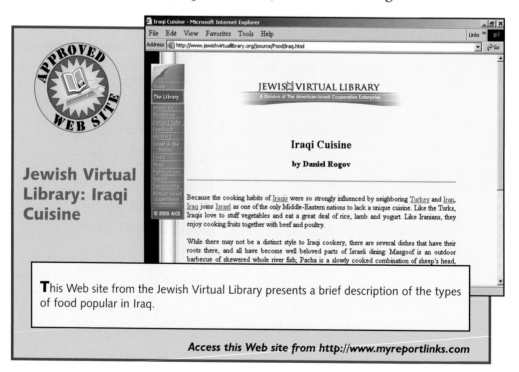

Jewish Virtual Library: Iraqi Cuisine

This Web site from the Jewish Virtual Library presents a brief description of the types of food popular in Iraq.

Access this Web site from http://www.myreportlinks.com

Uniquely Iraqi dishes include *masgoof,* an outdoor barbecue of skewed river fish. Another is *pacha,* a broth made out of sheep parts and various other meats. A grilled lamb dish, *quizi,* is stuffed with almonds, rice, spices, and raisins. A side-dish called *turshi* is made from a mixture of pickled vegetables.

Many of Iraq's devout Muslims eat strictly according to *halal;* dietary laws of Islam. Like Jews, deeply religious Iraqis do not eat pork. Nor do they eat any other meat that is not slaughtered according to Islamic ritual.

Although alcohol is forbidden by Islam, it can be bought legally in the country, and many Iraqis drink. A national form of vodka, *arrak,* is made from dates or grapes. Iraqis also make good quality beer and wine. Iraqis are enthusiastic tea drinkers who also occasionally enjoy coffee.[26]

Some Iraqi dishes have actually been imported from Europe. Back when Jews formed a significant part of Iraqi culture, a Jewish chef went to Italy and returned with the recipe for pizza. The Iraqi name for this still-popular dish is *lahma bi ajeen.*[27]

Early History

The land where civilization first appeared is called *Mesopotamia*. Three fourths of what was Mesopotamia lies within the borders of what is now Iraq. Mesopotamia means "land between two rivers," referring to the Tigris and Euphrates. Actually, the region extends outside of those rivers as well. The name Mesopotamia did not exist among the so-called Mesopotamian people, who sometimes referred to the region where they lived simply as "the Land." The name was created later by Greek historians.[1]

Southern Mesopotamia has always boasted the richest farmland in the Middle East. Even so, historians have pointed out that it was hardly an ideal place to start a civilization. Then, as today, the region was prone to terrible flooding. Moreover, it lacked metal, stone, and timber. Such materials, necessary for civilized arts and industry, had to be imported. Mesopotamia was also surrounded by deserts and mountains inhabited by hostile neighbors. Finally, it had little access to the sea. Nevertheless, the ancient Mesopotamians

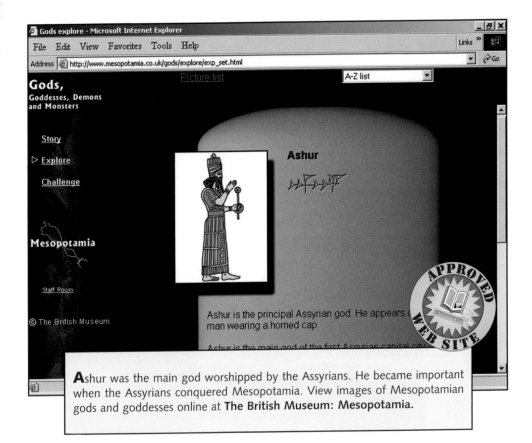

Gods, Goddesses, Demons and Monsters

Story

▷ Explore

Challenge

Mesopotamia

Staff Room

© The British Museum

Ashur

Ashur is the principal Assyrian god. He appears a man wearing a horned cap.

Ashur is the main god of the first Assyrian capital city

Ashur was the main god worshipped by the Assyrians. He became important when the Assyrians conquered Mesopotamia. View images of Mesopotamian gods and goddesses online at **The British Museum: Mesopotamia.**

achieved seeming miracles, building one civilization after another. Eventually, their region was taken over by a long line of other peoples.

Ancient Mesopotamia

Civilization dawned in Mesopotamia during the fourth millennium B.C. with the founding of Sumer. This was a group of city-states that included Uruk (the Erech of the Bible), Eridu, Kish, Lagash, Agade, Akshak, Larsa, and Ur. The Sumerians introduced many important ideas and inventions. They expanded irrigation and figured out how to make clay bricks for building. They also invented astronomy, numerical systems, and the wheel. Most important for the development of civilization, they invented writing.[2]

The earliest form of writing from Mesopotamia appeared around 3300 B.C. It consisted of crude little drawings called pictograms. By the middle of the third millennium B.C., the Sumerians had invented a full writing system that is now called cuneiform. It was written upon clay tablets using reeds with wedge-shaped tips.[3] Developed first solely for accounting purposes, writers of cuneiform

The British Museum: COMPASS Collection Online Web site gives a detailed look at this mask of the demon Huwawa. In the *Epic of Gilgamesh*, Huwawa is the guardian of the Cedar Forest. The demon is eventually defeated by Gilgamesh.

came to produce the earliest masterpieces of world literature, including *The Epic of Gilgamesh.*

This great poem tells the tragic story of its title character. A king of Ur, Gilgamesh begins as a cruel tyrant. He learns to rule justly, grieves the death of his friend Enkidu, and goes on a failed quest for eternal life. *The Epic of Gilgamesh* also includes a story of a worldwide flood. This story is strikingly similar to the biblical story of Noah, although it was written much earlier. Gilgamesh himself was a historical figure, a king who lived around 2700 B.C.[4]

The Sumerians were the first of a series of peoples who dominated the region. In about 2334 B.C., Akkadians came to power when King Sargon I conquered the Sumerians. Sending his armies as far away as Egypt and Ethiopia, Sargon built the world's first empire. Other peoples who came to power in the region included Amorites, Hittites, Assyrians, and Chaldeans.

One of Mesopotamia's most famous rulers was the Amorite king Hammurabi (1792–50 B.C.), who reigned in the city of Babylon. He created a set of laws known as the Code of Hammurabi. Although not actually ancient Mesopotamia's earliest known laws, these are the most complete.[5]

► Nebuchadrezzar II and Other Kings

Another famous ruler was the Chaldean king Nebuchadrezzar II (605–562 B.C.). He is notorious in the Bible for destroying Jerusalem and carrying the Hebrews into Babylonian captivity.[6] The spectacular Hanging Gardens of Babylon were said to have been built during his reign.

Ranked among the seven wonders of the ancient world by ancient historians, the Hanging Gardens were said to have grown on huge terraces raised upon columns. Massive machines supposedly raised water up to the gardens from the Euphrates.[7] It is now believed that descriptions of the gardens are at least somewhat false, and some question whether they existed.[8]

▲ Part of what remains of the Palace of Nebuchadrezzar in Babylon. This is located in what is now called Dur Sharrukin, Iraq, or Ancient Khorsabad.

In 539 B.C., Cyrus the Great of Ancient Persia conquered Babylon. The Bible tells how Cyrus released the Hebrews from Babylonian captivity to return to their homeland.[9] Cyrus's conquest led to two centuries of Persian rule over Mesopotamia.

Persian rule ended when Alexander the Great of Macedon conquered Babylon for Greece in 331 B.C. Alexander's conquest was followed by an era of Hellenistic (Greek) influence throughout Mesopotamia. Western religion, art, and ideas replaced older Mesopotamian ways.

A nomadic people called the Parthians then conquered Mesopotamia in 126 B.C. With the exception of two brief periods of Roman rule, the Parthians controlled the region until A.D. 227. In that year, Mesopotamia was conquered by Persian people called the Sassanids. During the rule of the Sassanids, the once-great Mesopotamian civilization fell into a steady decline.[10] The Sassanids ruled until A.D. 636.

▷ The Arrival of Islam

Islam came to the region in the seventh century. Muhammad's brother-in-law, Ali, won an important military victory in 655 near Basra, located in today's southeastern Iraq. There he asserted his claim to be Islam's fourth caliph (leader). For a time, Ali made the Iraqi city of Kufah the capital of Islam. He was assassinated in Kufah in A.D. 661.[11]

Ali's martyrdom led to the division of Islam into Shi'a and Sunni branches. Ali's son, Hussein, fought for the Shi'ite belief that only Muhammad's descendants could be caliphs. Hussein was defeated and killed in battle in 680 at Karbala, a city in central Iraq. He is buried at Karbala. His father, Ali, is buried at An Najaf, about seven miles from Kufah. Both of their graves are pilgrimage sites, almost as sacred to Shi'ites as the city of Mecca.[12]

In 747, Iraq was conquered by the Islamic leader Abu Muslim. This began the Abbasid dynasty, a line of Sunni caliphs who ruled the Islamic world from 750 until 1258. Al Mansur, the second Abbasid caliph, chose the little village of Baghdad as the capital of Islam.

Treasures From the Royal Tombs of Ur

The University of Pennsylvania Museum's Web site has an online exhibition of artifacts from the royal tombs from the Sumerian city of Ur. Ur is located in the southern part of present-day Iraq. View the collection from this exhibit on this site.

Access this Web site from http://www.myreportlinks.com

Within half a century, Baghdad became one of the world's most magnificent cities. It grew to be second in size only to Constantinople, then the capital of the Christian world. At its peak, Baghdad was a thriving hub of international trade. It was also the world's greatest center of arts, literature, philosophy, and science. All of the surrounding areas shared in Baghdad's glory.[13]

Iraq's greatest age ended with the arrival of the Mongols, invaders from the east. Led by Hulagu Khan, the Mongols seized Baghdad in 1258, killing the last of the Abbasid caliphs. Khan killed all of Baghdad's finest thinkers and inflicted fearful destruction upon the city. In 1401, another Mongol leader named Tamerlane spread death and ruin throughout Iraq. The region's greatest glory days were over.[14]

The Ottoman Empire

During the sixteenth century, two Islamic empires struggled for control of Iraq. These were the Iranian Safavid Empire and the Turkish Ottoman Empire. The Safavids seized Iraq in 1509, but the Ottomans took it away from them in 1535. The Safavids reconquered Baghdad in 1623, but lost it again to the Ottomans in 1638.

The Safavids were Shi'a Muslims, while the Ottomans were Sunni. As a result, these years of conflict increased the division between Shi'ites and Sunnis in Iraq—a division that continues today. After their victory in 1638, Ottomans controlled Iraq until the twentieth century. They placed local Sunnis in power, causing hardship and bitterness among the Shi'ites.[15]

By the sixteenth century, the Ottoman Empire was truly vast. It included Anatolia (present-day Turkey), all of the Middle East, parts of North Africa, and much of Eastern Europe, including Greece. But Ottoman control over its empire was often weak and indirect. In the region that is now Iraq, local tribes exercised increasing political power, often fighting among themselves. Tribal influence continues to affect Iraqi politics to this day.

▷ Westernizing Iraq

During the nineteenth century, the Ottoman leader Midhat Pasha tried to exert more control over Iraq. He was especially successful in bringing modern, Western ways to the region. Steamboats traveled the rivers, and telegraph lines spread throughout Iraq. Western-style capitalism grew, creating new opportunities for social mobility. Moreover, educational systems were run by the government and improved. This development produced a small but growing number of Iraqi intellectuals.

However, it is important to remember that the word Iraqi is used here loosely. Properly speaking,

▲ *These models are wearing traditional clothing from what was then known as the Baghdad province of the Ottoman Empire. This picture was taken in 1873.*

Iraq did not yet exist. Under the Ottoman Empire, today's Iraq consisted of three provinces surrounding the towns of Mosul, Baghdad, and Basra.[16] That situation would suddenly change early in the twentieth century.

Modern History

During the first years of the twentieth century, much of world stood at the brink of war. This conflict finally erupted over a single event—the killing of Austria's Archduke Francis Ferdinand by a Serbian assassin on June 28, 1914. Soon, countries everywhere were drawn into the Great War, better known today as World War I. Up to that time, it was the bloodiest conflict fought in human history.

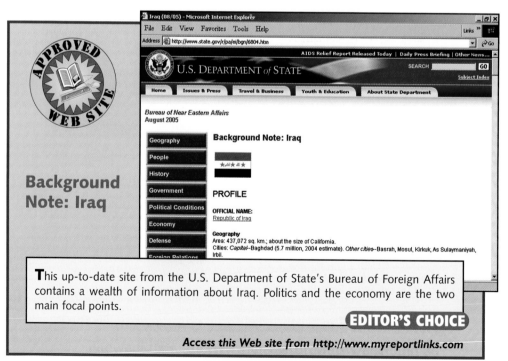

Background Note: Iraq

This up-to-date site from the U.S. Department of State's Bureau of Foreign Affairs contains a wealth of information about Iraq. Politics and the economy are the two main focal points.

EDITOR'S CHOICE

Access this Web site from http://www.myreportlinks.com

The war was between two groupings of countries—the Allies and the Central Powers. The Allies included France, Great Britain, Russia, Italy, and eventually the United States. The Central Powers included Germany, Austria-Hungary, Bulgaria, and the Turkish-ruled Ottoman Empire.

After the loss of millions of lives, the war ended in 1918 with an Allied victory. Among the many consequences of the war, the Ottoman Empire came to an end. Iraq was about to begin its troubled history as a nation.

The British Mandate

After the war, the League of Nations was formed. This was an international organization resembling today's United Nations. The league divided up territories formerly belonging to the Germans and Ottomans into nation-states called mandates. These were to be ruled, at least temporarily, by Allied countries. For example, Palestine became a British mandate, while Syria and Lebanon became French mandates.

The British had invaded and conquered the Ottoman provinces of Basra, Baghdad, and Mosul in 1914. Together, those provinces became a British mandate in 1919. They were then named after the Arabic term al-'Iraq, meaning farmland along a river's shore. At least since the A.D. 700s, the word had been used to refer to Mesopotamia's alluvial plains.[1]

As a nation, Iraq had never really existed before. Writes historian Charles Tripp, "The history of Iraq begins here, not simply as the history of the state's formal institutions, but as the histories of all those who found themselves drawn into the new regime of power."[2]

Trouble With the Mandate

The British quickly found the mandate of Iraq extremely difficult to manage. A full-scale rebellion broke out in 1920. Even the Sunnis and Shi'ites put their differences temporarily aside, joining together to fight for Iraqi independence. Lawlessness seized the country for three months. At last, the British succeeded in putting down the rebellion by military force.

After the rebellion ended, the British installed a monarchy—a government headed by a king. The first king of Iraq was Faisal, who was already an influential figure among Arabs. He was descended from the family of Muhammad and had briefly been Syria's king. Most importantly, the British felt sure that he would cooperate with their rule.

The British also granted political influence to the minority Sunnis. So, Sunnis dominated the majority Shi'ites, just as they had under Ottoman rule. This decision created difficulties that continue today.

Another long-lasting problem was created by the British mandate. In 1920, the League of Nations promised the Kurdish people their own homeland. This homeland would have consisted of the northeast province of Mosul and parts of neighboring countries where Kurds lived. But the league's promise was broken.

The British were anxious to keep the province of Mosul within their mandate. This was largely because the British suspected that oil might be found there.[3] Indeed, oil was discovered near the northeastern cities of Kirkuk and Mosul in the late 1920s. In 1925, the Mosul province became a permanent part of Iraq. Kurds were

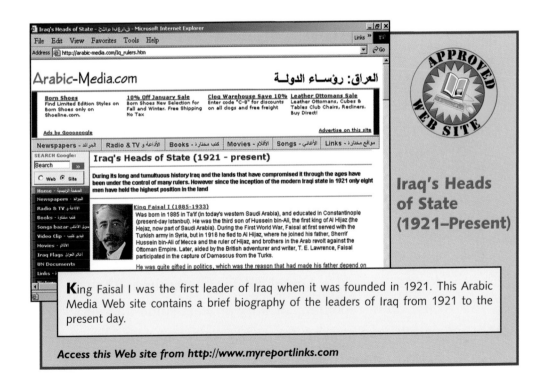

Iraq's Heads of State (1921–Present)

King Faisal I was the first leader of Iraq when it was founded in 1921. This Arabic Media Web site contains a brief biography of the leaders of Iraq from 1921 to the present day.

Access this Web site from http://www.myreportlinks.com

allowed to keep speaking their language in public and exercise some degree of self-government. Even so, they staged several rebellions against British rule.

Political developments in England finally ended the British mandate in Iraq. Britain's Labor party won the British election in 1929. The party was opposed to continuing the mandate. In 1932, Iraq joined the League of Nations and achieved independence. However, Great Britain continued to maintain a strong military presence in Iraq.

▷ Independence and Monarchy

King Faisal found himself in charge of an independent but restless country. Many factors made his reign difficult. For one thing, Iraq's boundaries had been artificially created by the British. As a result, there were instances of migration problems and skirmishes with neighboring countries.

Moreover, because he was installed by the British, King Faisal's legitimacy was doubted by many Iraqis. Therefore, he had trouble exerting royal authority. Several groups were especially troublesome. Sunnis and Shi'ites resumed their long-standing conflict. Iraq's Assyrians, like the Kurds, wanted a homeland for themselves. They rose up in rebellion, seeking at least some degree of self-government. Iraqi tribes also struggled for power under Faisal's regime.

King Faisal suddenly died of a heart attack in September 1933. An able leader despite the difficulties of his reign, Faisal was succeeded by his less experienced twenty-one-year-old son, Ghazi. Under Ghazi's rule, a number of coups (sudden political takeovers) led to a series of eight different governments.

Ghazi was killed in a car accident in 1939. He was succeeded by his infant son, Faisal II. Ghazi's cousin, Prince Amir Abd al Ilah, became the country's regent—an official who makes royal decisions until a king reaches maturity.

In 1939, World War II broke out. This time, the opposing powers were the Allied countries and the Axis countries. The Allies included France, Great Britain, and the United States. The Axis included Germany, Italy, and Japan.

World War II

At the beginning of World War II, Iraqis were divided in their loyalties. On one hand, a treaty still bound them to Great Britain. On the other hand, many Iraqis resented the continuing British military presence in Iraq. In 1941, a new coup brought anti-British Iraqi generals to power. They briefly overthrew the monarchy and staged a rebellion against the British.

The generals were quickly defeated, and the monarchy was restored. A pro-British government was put in power. But after the failed coup, fewer and fewer Iraqis approved of the monarchy. To many, Iraq's royal family seemed to be a way for the British to control the country.

In 1943, Iraq joined the Allies and declared war on the Axis powers. Iraq served as an important base of military operations in the Middle East. When the war ended in 1945, Iraq became part of the United Nations. This new international organization was created to replace the League of Nations, which was disbanded in 1946.

Increasingly bad times fell upon Iraq after World War II. The country shared the rest of the Arab world's outrage over the creation of the Jewish state of Israel in 1948. Iraq sent between

Country Profile: Iraq

This BBC site contains a brief overview of Iraq. Included are time lines of Iraq's history and key events for Iraqi Kurds.

Access this Web site from http://www.myreportlinks.com

eight thousand and ten thousand troops to fight in the Arab-Israeli War of that year. But the Arabs were defeated, and Iraqi troops fared especially badly. Moreover, the defeat further damaged Iraq's already troubled economy.

Poverty affected a growing number of Iraqis. Even a sudden increase in Iraq's oil production during the early 1950s did not help the average person. Corruption in high places kept ordinary Iraqi people from benefiting from oil profits. Protests against the Iraqi regime were common, sometimes turning violent. The government responded by declaring martial law and restricting political freedom.[4]

Iraqi Republic

Then, on July 14, 1958, Iraq's monarchy was overthrown. Led by rebel military officers, Iraqi soldiers seized Baghdad without a fight. The coup's leaders immediately declared Iraq a new republic. The young King Faisal II was executed, along with his regent, Amir Abd al Ilah, and many other members of the royal family.

Soon after the coup, military officer Abd al Karim Qasim became Iraq's prime minister, defense minister, and commander in chief. During his time in power, he made earnest efforts toward social justice. He redistributed land, empowered workers and peasants, and enacted programs to help the poor. He also founded the Iraq National Oil Company (INOC) in hopes of bringing oil profits to the Iraqi people.

Qasim's regime did not run smoothly, however. He frequently found himself at odds with powerful political forces. Iraq's Ba'ath party was especially hostile toward Qasim. In 1959, the Ba'athists decided that Qasim had to be killed. The assassination attempt was undertaken by Iraq's future dictator, Saddam Hussein. Though wounded, Qasim did not die. Even so, his hold on power weakened from that time on.

Kurdish Uprising

The Kurdish situation was one source of Qasim's problems. Upon the founding of the Republic of Iraq, the Kurdish people had been promised equal power with Iraqi Arabs. But Qasim failed to keep this promise, and a Kurdish uprising began in 1961. Qasim's failure to put down this rebellion stirred growing opposition to his government.

Qasim's political difficulties reached international levels. For example, the country of Kuwait declared its independence in 1961. Small, but rich in oil, Kuwait was situated along the southeast border of Iraq. Qasim denied Kuwaiti independence, insisting that the area belonged to Iraq. Because other Arab nations supported Kuwait, Qasim broke off diplomatic relations with them.

He found himself politically isolated not only within Iraq, but throughout the Arab world as well.[5]

▶ Ba'athist Takeover

Qasim was overthrown and executed by a Ba'athist coup in February 1963. The Ba'athists held power only briefly; they were overthrown by yet another coup in November 1963. Abd

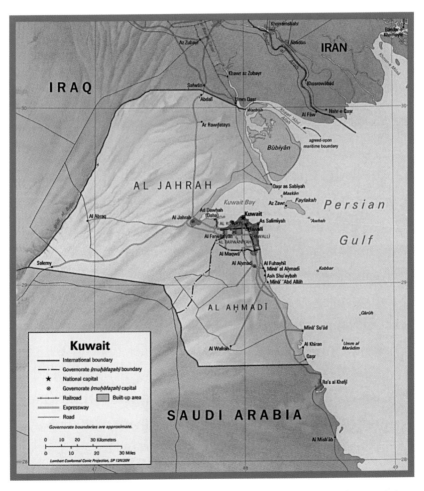

▲ Kuwait became an independent country in 1961. Immediately, Iraq did not approve of the Kuwaitis having their own country. This eventually led to the Persian Gulf War of 1991.

as Salaam Arif, one of the leaders of the 1958 revolution, became Iraq's new president.

Arif's government suffered from many of the same problems of earlier regimes. These included Kurdish rebellions and tense relations with other Arab countries. When Arif was killed in a helicopter crash in 1966, his brother, Abd ar Rahman Arif, became president. By then, the Iraqi government was badly weakened.

The 1967 Arab-Israeli War dealt a crowning blow to the Arif brothers' rule. During that six-day conflict, Israel soundly defeated Arab forces. The Jewish state also added the Gaza Strip, the Sinai Peninsula, the West Bank, and the Golan Heights to its territory. Iraqis thought it shameful that the Arif government was too feeble to lend assistance to the Arab cause in what came to be known as the Six-Day War. Iraqis' confidence in their government was completely lost.

The Rise of Saddam Hussein

In 1968, came yet another coup, overthrowing what was left of the Arif government. The socialist Ba'ath party seized power again—this time for good. The new Iraqi government was led by President Ahmad Hasan al Bakr. The Ba'ath party quickly showed its ruthlessness against anyone who challenged its rule. It staged sham trials and executed and assassinated its opponents.

Many of these harsh measures were carried out by Saddam Hussein, Bakr's cousin and right-hand man. Hussein was an ambitious young man of humble origins. He had been raised in a mud hut outside the Iraqi town of Tikrit.[6] Hussein's influence steadily rose in the Ba'ath regime. In fact, he quickly became more powerful than President Bakr himself.

Early Days of Hussein's Rule

Early on, Hussein proved himself a strangely contradictory leader. For example, he offered the Kurds the most generous autonomy (self-government) plan of any Iraqi government to date. At the same time, he forcibly relocated Kurds and introduced Arabs into their population. He also destroyed many Kurdish villages along the border of Iran.

However, Hussein did achieve some positive changes during his early years in power. He strengthened the economy, modernized industry, and distributed wealth more fairly. He also gave Iraqis greater access to education and health care. Perhaps most importantly, he created a stronger sense of national unity than Iraqis had ever known.

Finally, in 1979, Ahmad Hasan al Bakr resigned, and Hussein assumed absolute command as Iraq's president. Hussein asserted his brutality from the beginning of his rule. He is said to have executed some four hundred members of his own Ba'ath party soon after taking power.[7]

Years of War and Despair

By the time Saddam Hussein became president, relations were deeply strained between Iraq and its eastern neighbor Iran. Iraq and Iran had long disagreed over control of the Shatt al Arab River. Part of this short waterway lies on the Iraq-Iran border. The Shatt al Arab is extremely important to Iraq, because it offers the country's only access to the Persian Gulf. In 1975, however, Iraq had signed a treaty granting control of the Shatt al Arab to Iran. In exchange, Iran agreed to stop backing the Kurdish rebels in northern Iraq.

The final crisis in Iranian-Iraqi relations came in 1979, the year Hussein became president. That year, the ruling shah of Iran was deposed in an Islamic revolution. The radical cleric Ayatollah Ruhollah Khomeini then ruled a fundamentalist Shi'a government in Iran. Iraq's Sunni leaders felt threatened by this sudden development.

Hussein saw the crisis as an opportunity to assert Iraqi power in the region. In September 1980, he reclaimed control of the Shatt al Arab, despite the 1975 treaty. Later that month, he sent Iraqi forces to invade Iran. Iraq's initial invasion was successful. But a fierce Iranian counterattack drove Iraqi forces back. The war then dragged on for eight years.

▲ *A grieving mother kisses Saddam Hussein. Her son was killed on the frontlines of the Iran-Iraq War that lasted from 1980 to 1988.*

When the Iran-Iraq War began, the United States had its own problems with Khomeini's regime. Beginning on November 4, 1979, the Iranian government held 66 American diplomats hostage for 444 days. Not surprisingly, the United States government backed Hussein in his war against Iran. It supplied Iraq with intelligence and economic aid. Companies in Western countries—including the United States—sold Iraq materials for military use. Such companies also helped Iraq begin its notorious weapons of mass destruction (WMD) program.

An estimated one hundred thousand Iranians fell victim to Iraq's chemical weapons attacks. Hussein also used such weapons against the Kurdish people of his own country. The worst of these attacks occurred in the Kurdish city of Halabja in March 1988. At the time, the city was held by Iranian forces and Kurdish allies of Iran. Casualty estimates of the Halabja attack range from several hundred to five thousand people.

By the time the Iran-Iraq War ended, both countries had suffered terribly, and neither was the clear winner. Iraq had gained nothing from its

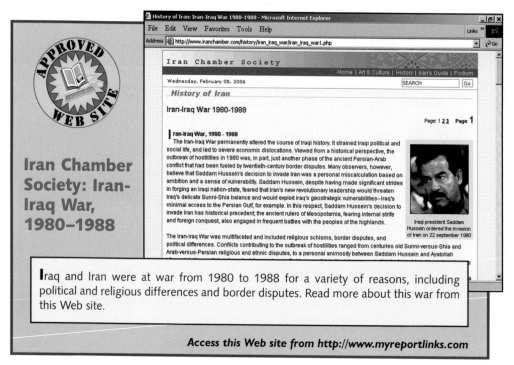

Iran Chamber Society: Iran-Iraq War, 1980–1988

Iraq and Iran were at war from 1980 to 1988 for a variety of reasons, including political and religious differences and border disputes. Read more about this war from this Web site.

Access this Web site from http://www.myreportlinks.com

aggression. It was forced to give up the rights to the Shatt al Arab River that it had claimed before the war. Worse, about a quarter of a million Iraqis had died.

In addition to the human tragedy of the conflict, Iraq was also weakened economically. In financing the war, Iraq ran up an international debt of about $80 billion. Creditor nations included Kuwait, long believed by many Iraqis to properly belong to their own country.

▶ The First Gulf War and Sanctions

In 1990, Hussein decided to invade and seize Kuwait. He hoped that this action would strengthen Iraq's fading power in the Arab world. On August 2, 1990, the invasion began. Within twenty-four hours, Iraq had conquered Kuwait. Within days, Kuwait was declared a province of Iraq.[8]

The conquest of Kuwait was a huge miscalculation on Hussein's part. The United Nations quickly condemned the invasion and imposed economic sanctions (bans on foreign trade) against Iraq. It also authorized the use of military force if Iraq failed to withdraw from Kuwait by January 15, 1991.[9]

The leaders of Saudi Arabia, Iraq's neighbor, worried that Iraq might invade their country next. So they asked the United States for military aid. This request led to the 1991 Persian Gulf War, in which United States-led forces liberated Kuwait.

On January 16, air strikes were launched against
Iraqi forces. This phase was quickly followed by
the use of ground troops, which led to a quick
victory. By March 3, the war was over.

Tens of thousands of Iraqis were killed in the
first Persian Gulf War. But still greater sufferings
lay ahead for Iraq's people. Much of the country's
infrastructure was destroyed by the allied invasion.

▲ This Iraqi tank was destroyed during the Persian Gulf War which lasted
from January to April 1991.

Moreover, the United Nations doubted that Iraq was cooperating with official demands that it get rid of its WMDs. Therefore, the UN did not lift its sanctions against Iraq. As a result, many people lacked basic necessities of life, including food and drinkable water. Perhaps the most reliable study of the sanctions disaster was made by public health specialist Richard Garfield. He determined that, between 1991 and 1998, 350,000 more children died in Iraq than would have under ordinary circumstances. The sanctions clearly played a role in this rise in child mortality.[10]

Corruption

Nevertheless, the sanctions failed to weaken Hussein's regime. He and others in power horded goods and services at the expense of the rest of Iraq's population. Moreover, Hussein used the sanctions for propaganda purposes. The hardships helped him to stir up anti-Western feeling and create a greater feeling of Iraqi unity. Some observers and historians believe that the sanctions made Hussein's regime even stronger.[11]

To relieve Iraq's humanitarian crisis, the UN began its Oil-for-Food Program in 1996. Its purpose was to allow Iraq to export oil in exchange for food, medicine, and other vital necessities. However, the program eventually proved to be riddled with corruption on the part of the Iraqi

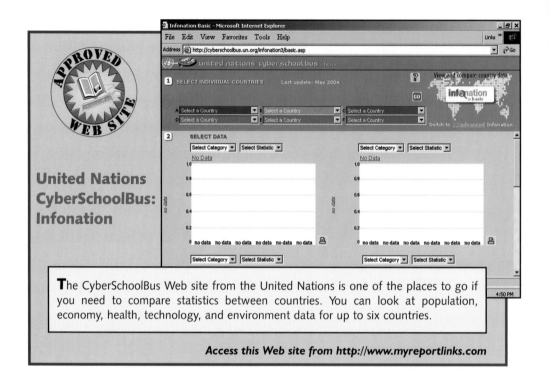

United Nations
CyberSchoolBus:
Infonation

The CyberSchoolBus Web site from the United Nations is one of the places to go if you need to compare statistics between countries. You can look at population, economy, health, technology, and environment data for up to six countries.

Access this Web site from http://www.myreportlinks.com

government and thousands of international companies.[12]

▶ Clashes Over Weapons

In 1997, Hussein expelled the UN inspection team searching for WMDs. From that time on, Western countries worried about whether Iraq possessed chemical and biological weapons. In 1998, the United States and Great Britain launched four days of air strikes against possible Iraqi weapons stockpiles.[13]

Then, on September 11, 2001, Islamic terrorists used passenger planes to attack the World Trade Center in New York and the Pentagon in

Washington, D.C. These attacks killed almost three thousand people. America then became more anxious than ever about terrorist attacks.

In his State of the Union address on January 29, 2002, President George W. Bush identified Iraq, Iran, and North Korea as an "axis of evil" bent on terrorizing the West. Bush promised not to allow "the world's most dangerous regimes to threaten us with the world's most destructive weapons."[14]

On November 18, 2002, UN weapons inspectors returned to Iraq. The team submitted its first report on January 27, 2003. The report doubted Iraq's cooperation with UN demands for disarmament. But another report submitted on February 14 suggested that progress toward disarmament was being made.[15]

The Fall of Hussein's Regime

In his second State of the Union speech on January 28, 2003, President Bush claimed that Iraq had tried to buy uranium to make nuclear weapons. He also announced his readiness to attack Iraq, with or without UN approval.

On February 5, 2003, U.S. Secretary of State Colin Powell followed up President Bush's threat in an appearance before the UN Security Council. There Powell presented evidence that Iraq had WMDs. He also argued that Iraq had

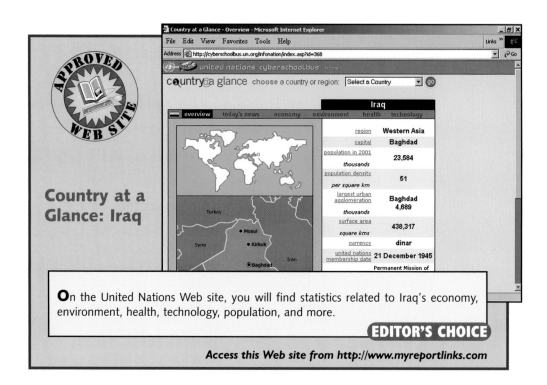

Country at a Glance: Iraq

On the United Nations Web site, you will find statistics related to Iraq's economy, environment, health, technology, population, and more.

EDITOR'S CHOICE

Access this Web site from http://www.myreportlinks.com

connections to al-Qaeda, the terrorist organization that had carried out the September 11 attacks.[16]

The United States' preparations for war against Iraq stirred controversy throughout the world. The United Nations refused to grant its approval. Indeed, after the invasion, UN Secretary-General Kofi Annan said, "From our point of view and the UN charter point of view, it was illegal."[17]

Despite the UN's objections, the United States and Great Britain assembled what they called the "coalition of the willing"—forty-nine countries that would contribute troops and support to the invasion. Notably absent from the coalition were important nations such as France, Germany, Russia, and China.[18]

Military action began on March 20, 2003. The coalition carried out the invasion remarkably quickly and easily. Iraq's capital city of Baghdad fell to coalition forces on April 9. Saddam Hussein's hometown of Tikrit was seized on April 14. On May 1, President Bush declared an end to major combat.[19]

Iraq in Transition

After the coalition victory, Saddam Hussein went into hiding. He had left a terrible mark on Iraq's history. Somewhere between 300,000 and 1.3 million people disappeared or were killed during his quarter century in power. Even members of Hussein's own family were not spared. At least two of his sons-in-law were probably murdered at his orders.[1]

Hussein's regime also commonly used terrible means of torture. For example, husbands were forced to watch their wives being raped, and parents had to watch their naked children stung by scorpions. Even after his fall from power, many Iraqis feared that he might return.[2]

With the end of his regime came the daunting task of rebuilding a shattered nation. After years of brutal dictatorship,

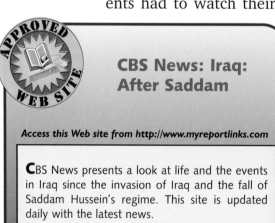

CBS News: Iraq: After Saddam

Access this Web site from http://www.myreportlinks.com

CBS News presents a look at life and the events in Iraq since the invasion of Iraq and the fall of Saddam Hussein's regime. This site is updated daily with the latest news.

failed and costly wars, and international sanctions, Iraq was in shambles. Many Iraqis had long lacked the basic necessities of life. Moreover, Saddam's fall posed the difficult question of how Iraqis might govern themselves.

▶ The Rising Insurrection

There were scenes of jubilation throughout Iraq during the victorious advance of coalition troops. The most famous of these took place on April 9, 2003, after the fall of Baghdad. Iraqis surrounded Hussein's huge statue in Baghdad's main square and unsuccessfully tried to topple it.

American troops arrived with a heavy armored vehicle and succeeded in pulling the statue to the ground. Iraqis then danced upon it and tore it to pieces. At last, they dragged its head through the streets by chains.

Even this joyful episode hinted at tensions to come. Before the statue was pulled down, a United States soldier placed an American flag over the statue's face. Iraqis were suddenly offended. The United States flag was hastily replaced by an Iraqi flag, and the crowd cheered again.[3]

The joy of the coalition victory soon faded. Coalition forces, mostly United States troops, occupied Iraq, placing it under foreign rule. An armed insurgency against the occupation quickly began. The violence of this rebellion continues to be fierce.

The insurgency consists of many different kinds of fighters with many different interests. Some of the insurgents are former followers of Saddam Hussein or people who prospered under his regime. Others are Islamic militants, either from Iraq or other countries. Still others are simply criminals fighting for money. Many of the insurgents are radical Sunnis. Their goal is to keep Shi'ites from taking control of a democratic Iraq.

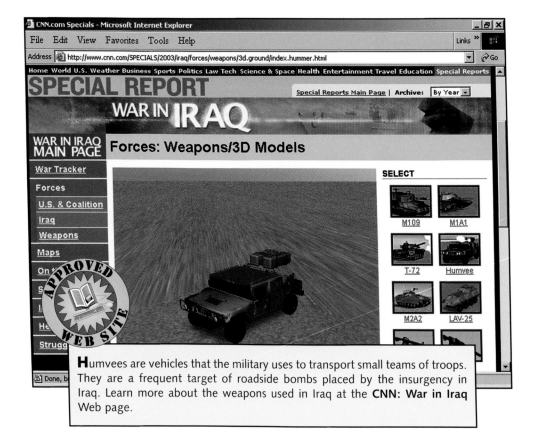

Humvees are vehicles that the military uses to transport small teams of troops. They are a frequent target of roadside bombs placed by the insurgency in Iraq. Learn more about the weapons used in Iraq at the **CNN: War in Iraq** Web page.

Some insurgents target coalition troops. They especially target United States soldiers. Others target Iraqi civilians, especially those who cooperate with the coalition's occupation of Iraq. Insurgents' methods vary widely. They include road bombs that destroy military vehicles, suicide bombings, kidnappings, and executions.

▷ Mounting Death Toll

The insurgency has taken a severe toll on United States forces and morale. During major combat operations, only 140 United States troops were killed. By February 12, 2006, that number had risen to 2,267, largely because of the insurgency.[4]

Attacks have also been terribly hard on the Iraqi people. The insurgency took on a chilling new focus on September 14, 2005. On that day, Abu Musab al-Zarqawi, an Iraq-based leader of the international terrorist organization al-Qaeda, declared war on Iraq's Shi'a majority. This declaration was followed by an increase in terrorist bombings targeting Iraqi Shi'ites.[5]

Iraq has suffered greatly since the coalition invasion. An independent study issued in October 2004 estimated that at least one hundred thousand Iraqi civilians had died because of coalition activities.[6] And now, the country is faced with the grim possibility of an all-out civil war between its Shi'a and Sunni populations.

Political Progress

While the insurrection grew, the original reasons for United States-led invasion of Iraq came into question. Before the war, the Bush administration had claimed that Hussein held WMDs and was trying to make nuclear weapons. It had also maintained that Iraq and al-Qaeda had cooperated in the September 11, 2001, attacks on America.

But President Bush's claim that Iraq had tried to purchase uranium for nuclear weapons proved to be based on faulty intelligence. Moreover, official investigations found no evidence of Iraq and al-Qaeda joining forces against America. By January 2005, the Bush administration conceded that no WMDs were to be found in Iraq.[7]

Little by little, the principal arguments made by the United States and Great Britain for the invasion were proven wrong. But another goal of the war remained intact. This was to create a stable, democratic Iraqi government, defended by a strong Iraqi security force. Such a government could serve as a beacon of freedom throughout the Arab world.

On July 13, 2003, the United States-led coalition established a temporary, limited government called the Iraqi Interim (transitional) Governing Council. Even the UN praised the council as "an important step towards the formation by the

▲ *These United States troops are waiting for the Iraqi forces to advance during Operation Iraqi Freedom.*

people of Iraq of an internationally recognized, representative government . . ."[8]

However, U.S. Ambassador Paul Bremer effectively remained Iraq's real leader. Pressure mounted for the coalition to turn governmental control of the nation over to the Iraqi people. This transfer took place on June 28, 2004. A transitional government led by Prime Minister Iyad Allawi then took power, and the Iraqi Interim Governing Council was dissolved.

January 27, 2005, brought Iraq's first free elections in fifty years. Iraqis chose a 275-seat National Assembly. Some 8.5 million Iraqis defied acts of insurgent violence and went to the polls. Due to a widespread boycott, only about 2 percent of eligible Sunnis voted.[9] Nevertheless, the election was regarded internationally as a major step toward Iraqi democracy. In April 2005, the newly elected National Assembly chose Kurdish leader Jalal Talabani as Iraq's new president.

The primary goal of the National Assembly was to produce a new constitution. A draft of this document was presented to the Iraqi people at the end of August 2005. Another election was held on October 15 in which Iraqis voted on whether to accept the constitution. The document was upheld by 79 percent of the voters. This election was marked by greater Sunni participation than the election in January. Although the majority of Sunnis voted against the constitution, many now felt it necessary to participate in the democratic process.

The Iraqi constitution as it is currently written raises unsettling questions. Observers both inside and outside of Iraq worry that it will ultimately break up rather

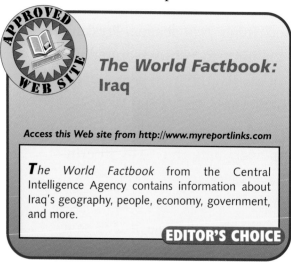

The World Factbook: Iraq

Access this Web site from http://www.myreportlinks.com

The World Factbook from the Central Intelligence Agency contains information about Iraq's geography, people, economy, government, and more.

EDITOR'S CHOICE

than unify the country. Instead of a strong central government, the constitution grants independent power to Iraq's three main regions. These are the Kurdish north, the Shi'a south, and the central Sunni region surrounding Baghdad.

The Sunnis, once the most powerful group in Iraq, would suffer from such a breakup. While both the Kurdish and Shi'a regions are rich in petroleum, there is virtually no oil in the Sunni region. Understandably, Sunnis prefer a strong central government in which they can share power with Kurds and Shi'ites.

But the constitution remains a work in progress. By continuing to participate in the political process, an increasing number of Sunnis hope to revise the document to reflect their own interests.[10]

Hussein Brought to Justice

While post-invasion events unfolded in Iraq, Saddam Hussein himself emerged to play an oddly minor role. On December 13, 2003, American troops found and captured the deposed dictator. He was hiding in a hole near his hometown of Tikrit.

On October 19, 2005, Hussein and several political accomplices went on trial before an Iraqi court. They stood accused of mass murder. Hussein appeared defiant, but pathetic in some ways. Caged with his codefendants in the courtroom,

http://images.wn.com/i/b2/a120bf74159b41.jpg - Microsoft Internet Explorer

File   Edit   View   Favorites   Tools   Help   Links »

Address http://images.wn.com/i/b2/a120bf74159b41.jpg   Go

On October 19, 2005, Saddam Hussein began his trial for war crimes. Among the things he is accused of is gassing Kurds to death with chemical weapons. This image can be found on the *Iraq Daily* Web site.

Hussein insisted that he was still president of Iraq. He also denied the authority of the court.

Hussein may face the death penalty for the charges brought against him. However, on the first day of the trial, many Baghdad citizens seemed indifferent to the former dictator's fate. They were more worried about the threat of civil war and the continued lack of electricity and water.[11]

The Economy

By 1980, Iraq's economy had become the second largest in the Arab world and the third largest in the Middle East. In those days, Saddam Hussein managed the nation's business ruthlessly but effectively. However, during the two decades that followed, the economy was worn down by many factors. These included wars, increasing international isolation, and the UN sanctions of the 1990s.

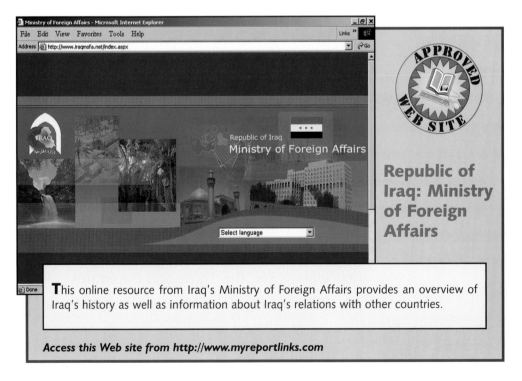

Republic of Iraq: Ministry of Foreign Affairs

This online resource from Iraq's Ministry of Foreign Affairs provides an overview of Iraq's history as well as information about Iraq's relations with other countries.

Access this Web site from http://www.myreportlinks.com

Because of Iraq's isolation, little was known of the country's economy during the 1990s. But after the United States-led coalition toppled Hussein in 2003, the international community found Iraq in economic shambles. The economy had shrunk during the last several years and it was expected to shrink a further 22 percent before the end of 2003. Average income had fallen from $2,600 per person in 1980 to between $450 and $610 at the end of 2003. Unemployment had reached an estimated 50 percent.

Moreover, about 30 percent of the workforce was employed by the government. And more than half the population depended on government food aid.[1] Worst of all, much of Iraq's water, electric, and sanitation systems were in ruin, with many Iraqis lacking the basic necessities of life.

After the war, it became the international community's daunting responsibility to help Iraqis restore their shattered economy.

▶ Agriculture and Fishing

Agriculture and fishing make up only a small part of Iraq's economy. This may seem surprising, since the region has been famous since ancient times for its two great waterways, the Tigris and Euphrates rivers, and the rich alluvial plains surrounding them. There is also good farmland among the steppes and foothills of the northern highlands.

Iraq, though, is mostly desert, leaving only about one fifth of the country's land suitable for farming. Irrigation also adds to the problem. Although it is necessary for planting on the alluvial plains, it also deposits salt that ruins the soil. Moreover, Iraqi agriculture has been impaired by the migration of many people from the countryside to cities like Baghdad.

All told, agriculture only accounts for one quarter to one third of Iraq's gross domestic product (GDP)—the total worth of the products and services that the people of a country create. Fishing accounts for only a tiny part of the GDP.

△ Oil is one of Iraq's greatest money-making resources. Unfortunately, the oil fields are often a target of insurgents who wish to cripple the flow of oil that mainly goes to Western nations.

Iraq's most important grains are wheat and barley. Among the country's vegetables are tomatoes, beans, eggplant, okra, cucumbers, and onions. Fruits include melons, grapes, apples, apricots, and citrus. Tobacco and cotton are also grown. Dates, which grow on palm trees, are Iraq's most important crop and a basic staple of Iraqis' diets. Domestic animals are raised in various parts of the country. These include sheep, goats, cattle, water buffalo, horses, and camels.

A few fishermen work along Iraq's tiny Persian Gulf coastline. Most of Iraq's fishing is done in inland waters—rivers, streams, lakes, and fish farms. Freshwater fish include mullet, catfish, and several varieties of carp.

▷ Petroleum

Iraq is estimated to hold 115 billion barrels of known oil reserves—the third largest in the world after Saudi Arabia and Canada. Much more oil may yet be found in unexplored parts of the country.[2] Not surprisingly, petroleum production makes up the single largest portion of Iraq's GDP.

The first oil fields in Iraq were discovered in 1927 near Kirkuk, and more oil was found soon afterward near Mosul. Both Kirkuk and Mosul remain major oil centers today. About 65 percent of all of Iraq's oil reserves are found in the southeast. Many of them are not far from the city of Basra.

During much of Iraq's history as a nation, its oil was largely controlled by foreign companies. But between 1972 and 1975, Iraq nationalized the industry—that is, put it under state ownership. Since then, the country's oil has been controlled by the Iraq National Oil Company (INOC).

CNN: World/Middle East

Access this Web site from http://www.myreportlinks.com

On the CNN Web site, you can read the top news stories from the Middle East, including Iraq.

The importance of oil to Iraq's economy became starkly clear during the UN sanctions of the 1990s. Virtually all Iraqi oil exports were stopped by the sanctions. As a result, Iraqis suffered a terrible humanitarian disaster in which hundreds of thousands of people were believed to have died. The UN's Oil-for-Food Program relieved this crisis somewhat.

Even so, Iraq's petroleum industry remains troubled today. Corruption, mismanagement, and outdated production methods limit both oil production and profits. As late as 2004, Iraq still had to import oil for its own uses.

Moreover, some experts worry about Iraq's future reliance on an economy based solely on oil. According to post-conflict resolution expert Bathsheba Crocker, such an economy can lead to "violent conflict, low economic growth, poor human development indicators, bad governance, and human rights abuses."[3]

Manufacturing and Industry

In addition to petroleum, Iraq's manufactured goods include aluminum, cement, detergents, electrical goods, steel, telephone cables, textiles, tires, and tractors.

Iraq's manufacturing capacities weakened during long years of war. This was especially true during the UN sanctions of the 1990s. However, manufacturing has rebounded since the UN's Oil-for-Food program was put in effect in 1996. By the end of the decade, almost all of Iraq's factories were running again, although they were somewhat less productive than in earlier years.[4]

Transportation and Telecommunications

Modes of travel in Iraq range from camels and horses to trains and jet planes. Iraq's transportation system has survived years of war surprisingly well. Rivers, lakes, and channels have long been used for navigation. The countryside is crossed with roads and railroads, which connect Iraq with neighboring countries. Iraq also has an extensive railway system, two international airports, and an airline.

Maureen Smith, a member of the U.S. Hospital Corps, gives medical care to an Iraqi baby.

Iraq's communication networks shrank during the hard years of Hussein's regime. Most Iraqis had no access to television, telephones, or radio. All television and radio broadcasts were controlled by the government. But telecommunications are swiftly rebounding in Iraq. Satellite television service is now available, as are cellular phones. Internet cafés are also springing up all over the country.

Looking Ahead

Under Saddam Hussein's socialist regime, Iraq had a command economy—one that was completely controlled by the state. Now that Hussein has fallen, many people hope that Iraq will develop a market economy—one in which buyers and sellers are free to make their own decisions. Companies that want to invest in Iraq's economic future are eager to see a market economy develop there.

Hopes for a market economy were especially high immediately after the coalition invasion. U.S. ambassador L. Paul Bremer III, then Iraq's temporary leader, announced in May 2003, "Iraq is open for business."[5]

Future Investment

Bremer's call for investors to pour money into Iraq amounted to little, however. International companies did not rush into Iraq to invest in the country's future. Potential investors were cautious for three reasons.

First, they were anxious about Iraq's security issues. A dangerous insurgency was underway, threatening not just coalition soldiers and Iraqi citizens, but foreigners hoping to do business in Iraq. Second, Iraq had no permanent government, causing investors to worry that contracts and agreements had no lasting legality. Third, investors could not be sure that Iraqis themselves shared international hopes for a market economy.

As Bathsheba Crocker put it, "Nothing guarantees that an elected Iraqi government will not . . . keep Iraq's economy closer in line with what it was historically, which included a nationalistic bias against foreign ownership."[6]

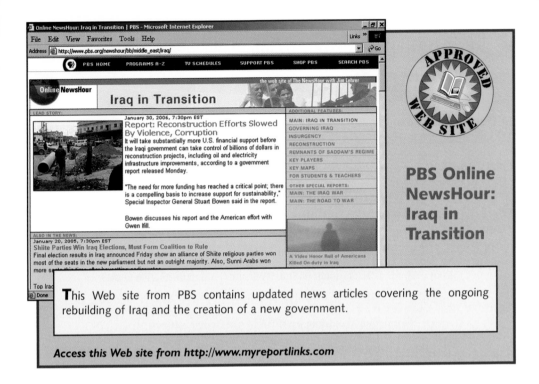

Online NewsHour: Iraq in Transition | PBS - Microsoft Internet Explorer

File Edit View Favorites Tools Help

Address http://www.pbs.org/newshour/bb/middle_east/iraq/

PBS HOME   PROGRAMS A-Z   TV SCHEDULES   SUPPORT PBS   SHOP PBS   SEARCH PBS

Online NewsHour

the web site of The NewsHour with Jim Lehrer

Iraq in Transition

LEAD STORY:

January 30, 2006, 7:30pm EST
Report: Reconstruction Efforts Slowed
By Violence, Corruption
It will take substantially more U.S. financial support before
the Iraqi government can take control of billions of dollars in
reconstruction projects, including oil and electricity
infrastructure improvements, according to a government
report released Monday.

"The need for more funding has reached a critical point; there
is a compelling basis to increase support for sustainability,"
Special Inspector General Stuart Bowen said in the report.

Bowen discusses his report and the American effort with
Gwen Ifill.

ADDITIONAL FEATURES:

MAIN: IRAQ IN TRANSITION
GOVERNING IRAQ
INSURGENCY
RECONSTRUCTION
REMNANTS OF SADDAM'S REGIME
KEY PLAYERS
KEY MAPS
FOR STUDENTS & TEACHERS
OTHER SPECIAL REPORTS:
MAIN: THE IRAQ WAR
MAIN: THE ROAD TO WAR

ALSO IN THE NEWS:
January 20, 2005, 7:30pm EST
Shiite Parties Win Iraq Elections, Must Form Coalition to Rule
Final election results in Iraq announced Friday show an alliance of Shiite religious parties won
most of the seats in the new parliament but not an outright majority. Also, Sunni Arabs won
more seats this time as few boycotted as discontent

A Video Honor Roll of Americans
Killed On-duty in Iraq

Top Iraq

Done

**PBS Online
NewsHour:
Iraq in
Transition**

This Web site from PBS contains updated news articles covering the ongoing
rebuilding of Iraq and the creation of a new government.

Access this Web site from http://www.myreportlinks.com

Iraq remains a nation largely in political, economic, and physical ruins. Iraqis and foreigners must share in the task of rebuilding the nation. The United States is especially determined that Iraq become fully democratic. But such a hope is double-edged. In a democracy, people make their own choices. And the world does not yet know what sort of future Iraqis will choose—one that promotes Western ways while recognizing Islam's traditional values, or one that reaches back into the Middle East's troubled past.

Report Links

The Internet sites described below can be accessed at http://www.myreportlinks.com

▶**The World Factbook: Iraq**
Editor's Choice Learn more about Iraq from this CIA Web site.

▶**In Depth: The Struggle For Iraq**
Editor's Choice Find out the latest news about the rebuilding of Iraq.

▶**CNN.com: Saddam Hussein on Trial**
Editor's Choice On this Web site from CNN, you can follow the trial of Saddam Hussein.

▶**Perry-Castañeda Library Map Collection: Iraq Maps**
Editor's Choice View historical and present-day maps of Iraq.

▶**Background Note: Iraq**
Editor's Choice The U.S. Department of State Web site has an informative section on Iraq.

▶**Country at a Glance: Iraq**
Editor's Choice Information about Iraq provided by the United Nations.

▶**Arab.net: Iraq**
This Web site provides general information on Iraq.

▶**Background Note: Iran**
Learn about Iraq's neighbor country.

▶**BBC News: Middle East**
Get the latest news from the Middle East.

▶**The British Museum: COMPASS Collection Online**
Explore the collections of the British Museum for artifacts from the Iraqi region.

▶**The British Museum: Mesopotamia**
Learn more about the region once known as Mesopotamia.

▶**CBS News: Iraq: After Saddam**
This Web site provides a comprehensive look at events since the fall of Saddam Hussein.

▶**CNN: War in Iraq**
Learn more about the war in Iraq on this site.

▶**CNN: World/Middle East**
Read the latest news from Iraq and the Middle East.

▶**Country Profile: Iraq**
The BBC provides an overview of this Middle Eastern country.

Tools   Search   Notes   Discuss

MyReportLinks.com Books

Go!

Report Links

The Internet sites described below can be accessed at
http://www.myreportlinks.com

▶**ESPN: Blood on the Rings**
An article from ESPN about Uday Hussein and the Iraqi National Olympic Committee.

▶*Frontline*/World: Iraq: **Truth and Lies in Baghdad, November 2002**
This Web site from PBS takes a look inside Iraq in November 2002.

▶**GlobalSecurity.org: Religious Structures**
Learn about the religious groups that are present in Iraq.

▶**Iran Chamber Society: Iran-Iraq War, 1980–1988**
Find out about the war between Iraq and Iran.

▶*Iraq Daily*
National and international news articles are on this daily Iraqi news site.

▶**Iraq's Heads of State (1921–Present)**
Read about the leaders of Iraq.

▶**Jewish Virtual Library: Iraqi Cuisine**
A brief overview of food in Iraq.

▶**Minnesota State University: Islam**
Learn the basics of Islam.

▶**PBS Online NewsHour: Iraq in Transition**
Up-to-date news articles about the rebuilding of Iraq.

▶**Republic of Iraq: Ministry of Foreign Affairs**
The official Web site from the Iraqi Ministry of Foreign Affairs.

▶**Strokes of Genius: Contemporary Iraqi Art**
View an exhibit of artwork from young Iraqi artists.

▶**Treasures from the Royal Tombs of Ur**
An online exhibition showcasing artifacts found in southern Iraq.

▶**United Nations CyberSchoolBus: Infonation**
The United Nations provides statistics on countries from around the world.

▶**Wars and Conflict: Iraq: Conflict in Context**
This Web site contains interesting information on Iraq's past.

▶**The White House: Renewal in Iraq**
The official White House Web site provides a look at the progress made in Iraq.

alluvial plains—A surface area laid down by streams, generally during flooding.

al-Qaeda—An international terrorist organization that now has insurgents in Iraq.

Arab—A large Middle-Eastern ethnic and cultural group; largely followers of Islam.

archaeology—The scientific study of prehistoric people and their cultures.

artifacts—Objects made by human beings.

autonomy—Political independence; self-government.

beit—"House;" a group of families within a tribe.

bilingual—Able to speak two languages.

boycott—Refusal to deal with an organization in protest against its policies.

cleric—A clergyman or other religious leader.

coalition—An organization of countries or people joined by treaty or agreement.

coup—A sudden change of government by force.

ethnicity—Distinctive cultural traits shared by a group.

extended family—A family consisting of parents and children plus other blood relatives such as grandparents, aunts, uncles, and cousins.

fakhdh—A tribal clan.

infidel—Someone who does not hold the same religious beliefs as the speaker or writer.

infrastructure—The public facilities, services, and equipment a country or area needs to function, such as water, power, and transportation.

insurgency—An uprising in rebellion against a government.

interim—Serving temporarily until a replacement can be made.

irrigation—Bringing water to a dry area, especially to farmlands.

kham—An extended family.

Kurds—An ethnic group inhabiting the northern part of Iraq and several neighboring countries.

League of Nations—An organization of nations formed in 1919 to promote cooperation and peace among nations.

millennium—A period of a thousand years.

monotheism—The belief that there is only one God.

nomads—Peoples who move from one place to another.

nuclear family—A family unit consisting of a mother, father, and their children.

pagan—A person who does not believe in Christianity, Judaism, or Islam.

patriarchal—Description of a culture in which the men are the most powerful members.

pilgrimage—A journey to a holy place for religious reasons.

polytheism—The belief in more than one god or supernatural being.

propaganda—Information spread to promote or to discredit a particular idea or cause, sometimes using deceptive information.

qabila—A federation (organization) of tribes.

regime—The governing authority; a system or style of government.

revelation—The revealing of something enlightening or astonishing; the communication of knowledge by a supernatural source.

sanctions—Measures adopted by a country or group of countries against another nation as punishment for breaking a rule or law.

secular—Not controlled by a religious body or based on religious beliefs.

shaikh—An Arab chief, especially of a tribe.

Sharia—Islamic law.

Shi'ite—The second-largest branch of Islam; the majority in Iraq.

shroud—A cloth that a dead body is wrapped in before burial.

skirmish—A brief fight between small groups.

steppes—Large area of land with grass but no trees.

Sunni—The largest branch of Islam; a minority in Iraq.

symbolize—To stand for, represent, or identify something else.

theocracy—A government led by a god, by priests, or by officials believed to be divinely guided.

United Nations (UN)—An organization of nations formed in 1945 to promote international peace, security, and cooperation.

Iraq Facts

1. All of this information is from the CIA *World Factbook,* "Iraq," *The World Factbook,* October 25, 2005, <http://www .cia.gov/cia/publications/factbook/geos/iz.html#Geo> (February 12, 2006).

Chapter 1. Iraq in the News

1. Michael Howard, "Mother Votes After Burying Her Son: Kirkuk Kurds Robbed of Their Homes Show Defiance, *The Guardian,* January 31, 2005, <http://www.guardian.co.uk/ Iraq/Story/0,2763,1402263,00.html> (October 11, 2005).

2. Matt Spetalnick, "Zarqawi Declares War on Election," *Yahoo! News: UK and Ireland,* January 23, 2005, <http://uk .news.yahoo.com/050123/325/favg4.html> (October 27, 2005).

3. Dexter Filkins, "Insurgents Vowing to Kill Iraqis Who Brave the Polls on Sunday," *NYTimes.com,* January 26, 2005, <http:// www.nytimes.com/2005/01/26/international/middleeast/ 26iraq.html?ex=1264395600&en=4f19f967c46be7b2&ei =5090&partner=rssuserland> (October 27, 2005).

4. Patrick B. Baetjer, "Iraqi Security and Military Force Developments: A Chronology," *Center for Strategic and International Studies,* February 16, 2005, <http://66.102.7 .104/search?q=cache:jHCrG0FlGFMJ:www.csis.org/features/ 041201_SecurityForcesTimeline.pdf+%22Iraqi+Security+and +Military+Force+Developments:+A+Chronology%22&hl= en&ie=UTF-8> (October 27, 2005).

5. Christiane Amanpour, et al, "Sporadic Violence Doesn't Deter Iraqi Voters," *CNN.com,* January 31, 2005, <http: //edition.cnn.com/2005/WORLD/meast/01/30/iraq.main/> (October 27, 2005).

6. "Elections Hailed a Success by the International Community (2005)," *Global IDP,* n.d., <http://www .db.idpproject.org/Sites/idpSurvey.nsf/wViewCountries/ B2B4B33E4A59DABAC1257013003EAD45> (October 27, 2005).

Chapter 2. Land and Climate

1. Central Intelligence Agency, "Iraq," *The World Factbook,* January 10, 2006, <http://www.cia.gov/cia/publications/ factbook/geos/iz.html#Geo> (February 12, 2006).

2. "Case Study: Iraq," *CBD (non)Proliferation Educational Module,* 1998–2001, <http://cbw.sipri.se/cbw/002020100 .html> (October 27, 2005).

3. Farouk El-Baz, "Iraq's Desert Also Needs Healing," *Geotimes,* June 2003, <http://www.geotimes.org/june03/ comment.html> (October 27, 2005).

4. Georges Roux, *Ancient Iraq,* 3rd ed. (London: Penguin Books, 1992), pp. 48–53.

5. David Minor, "A Canal Chronology," *Eagles Byte Historical Research,* July 1996, <http://home.eznet.net/~dminor/ Canals.html> (October 28, 2005).

6. Roux, p. 7.

7. "Water Returns to Iraqi Marshlands," *BBC News,* August 24, 2005, <http://news.bbc.co.uk/2/hi/science/nature/ 4177852.stm> (October 28, 2005).

8. Robert Fisk, "Their Lagoons and Reedbeds Gone, Iraq's Marsh Arabs Have No Refuge," *Common Dreams News Center,* September 12, 2005, <http://www.commondreams.org/ views01/0519-02.htm> (October 28, 2005).

9. "Water Returns to Iraqi Marshlands."

Chapter 3. Religion

1. Central Intelligence Agency, "Iraq," *The World Factbook,* January 10, 2006, <http://www.cia.gov/cia/publications/ factbook/geos/iz.html#Geo> (February 12, 2006).

2. Charles Tripp, *A History of Iraq* (Cambridge: Cambridge University Press, 2001), pp. 105–106.

3. Tore Kjeilen, "Iraq: Religions and Peoples," *Encyclopedia of the Orient,* 1996–2006, <http://i-cias.com/e.o/iraq_4 .htm> (October 28, 2005).

4 Hope For You, "Islam," *30 Days Muslim Prayer Focus,* 2002, <http://www.hfe.org/_old/prayer/ramadan/islam .htm> (October 28, 2005).

5. "Islam: Subdivisions: Sunni and Shia," *bbc.co.uk,* n.d., <http://www.bbc.co.uk/religion/religions/islam/subdivisions/ sunni_shia/> (October 28, 2005).

6. U.S. Library of Congress, "Islam," *Country Studies: Iraq,* n.d., <http://countrystudies.us/iraq/35.htm> (October 28, 2005).

7. "Outline of Differences Between Shi'ite and Sunni Schools of Thought," *Al-Islam.org,* n.d., <http://www .al-islam.org/encyclopedia/chapter9/1.html> (October 28, 2005).

8. Central Intelligence Agency, "Iraq."

9. Tripp, p. 12.

10. Ibid., p. 31.

11. "Text of the Draft Iraqi Constitution," *BBC News,* August 24, 2005, <news.bbc.co.uk/1/shared/bsp/hi/pdfs/24_08_05 _constit.pdf> (October 28, 2005).

12. The Everything Development Company, "Saudi Arabia," *Everything2.com,* n.d., <http://www.everything2.com/index .pl?node=Saudi%20Arabia> (October 28, 2005).

13. "Some of the Restrictions Imposed by Taliban on Women in Afghanistan," *Revolutionary Association of the Women of Afghanistan (RAWA),* n.d., <http://www.rawa .org/rules.htm> (October 28, 2005).

14. Lydia Ratna, "Women's Rights in Iraq," *Religion Beat,* May 27, 2003, <http://courses.washington.edu/com361/ Iraq/religion/women_iraq.html> (October 28, 2005).

Chapter 4. Iraqi Culture

1. Aisha El-Awady, "The Plunder of Iraq's Heritage," *IslamOnline.net,* March 29, 2003, <http://www.islamonline .net/English/artculture/2003/04/article08.shtml> (October 10, 2005).

2. Georges Roux, *Ancient Iraq,* 3rd ed. (London: Penguin Books, 1992), p 2.

3. El-Awady, "The Plunder of Iraq's Heritage."

4. Joanne Farchakh, "Restoring Baghdad's Museum to Its Former Glory," *The Daily Star,* October 8, 2004, <http:// www.dailystar.com.lb/article.asp?edition_id=10&categ_id= 4&article_id=9069> (October 28, 2005).

5. Noshir H. Dadrawala, "Yezidism," *Metareligion,* n.d., <http://www.meta-religion.com/World_Religions/yezidism.htm> (October 28, 2005)

6. Central Intelligence Agency, "Iraq," *The World Factbook,* January 10, 2006, <http://www.cia.gov/cia/publications/factbook/geos/iz.html#Geo> (February 12, 2006).

7. Tore Kjeilen, "Arabs," *Encyclopedia of the Orient,* 1996–2006, <http://i-cias.com/e.o/arabs.htm> (October 28, 2005).

8. Central Intelligence Agency, "Iraq."

9. Charles Tripp, *A History of Iraq* (Cambridge: Cambridge University Press, 2001), p. 244.

10. Ibid., pp. 197–198.

11. "Iraq—In Their Language," *CountryReports.Org,* 2005, <http://www.countryreports.org/greetings.aspx?countryid=117&countryName=Iraq&m=b> (October 4, 2005).

12. "Country Analysis Briefs: Iraq," *Energy Information Commission,* n.d., <http://www.eia.doe.gov/emeu/cabs/iraq.html> (October 28, 2005).

13. "Iraq: Family," *CountryReports.Org,* 2005, <http://www.countryreports.org/socializing.aspx?countryid=117&countryName=Iraq&m=b> (October 6, 2005).

14. Tripp, p. 65.

15. Hadani Ditmars, "The Arts in Iraq: Pretty, and Pretty Banal Post-Invasion: After Surrealism of War, Iraqi Artists Play it Safe," *SFGate.com,* December 7, 2003, <http://www.sfgate.com/cgi-bin/article.cgi?file=/chronicle/archive/2003/12/07/ING053E1UG1.DTL&type=printable> (October 28, 2005).

16. U.S. Library of Congress, "Education and Welfare," *Country Studies: Iraq,* n.d., <http://countrystudies.us/iraq/45.htm> (October 28, 2005).

17. Ibid.

18. Brian Whitaker, "Getting a Bad Press," *Guardian Unlimited,* June 23, 2003, <http://www.guardian.co.uk/elsewhere/journalist/story/0,7792,983342,00.html> (October 28, 2005).

19. Roshan Muhammed Salih, "Iraq's Media Failing Its Audience," *Aljazeera.net,* March 27, 2004, <http://english .aljazeera.net/NR/exeres/47BAC7B2-B10E-48AF-80FA-04CCF60A4FED.htm> (October 28, 2005).

20. Whitaker, "Getting a Bad Press."

21. Salih, "Iraq's Media Failing Its Audience."

22. IJNet, "New Media NGO Aims to Improve Iraqi Journalism," *Iraq Media Developments,* August 22, 2005, <http://www.stanhopecentre.org/blogs/iraqmedia/> (October 7, 2005).

23. Philip Sherwell, "On Eve of Olympics, Iraq Reveals How Uday Got Results," *news.telegraph,* July 25, 2004, <http:// www.telegraph.co.uk/news/main.jhtml?xml=/news/2004/07 /25/wirq25.xml&sSheet=/news/2004/07/25/ixnewstop.html> (October 9, 2005).

24. "Uday Hussein," *news.telegraph,* July 24, 2004, <http://www.telegraph.co.uk/news/main.jhtml;jsessionid= FQV0O02TNHRVBQFIQMGSM54AVCBQWJVC?xml=/news /2003/07/24/db2401.xml> (October 8, 2005)

25. The Cultural Orientation Project, "Some Cultural Differences," *culturalorientation.net,* February 18, 2004, <http://www.culturalorientation.net/Iraqi/icult.html> (February 12, 2006).

26. hunterV, "Baghdad: Local Customs Reviews," *VirtualTourist.com,* <http://www.virtualtourist.com/travel/ Middle_East/Iraq/Muhafazat_Baghdad/Baghdad-1796771/ Local_Customs-Baghdad-BR-1.html> (February 12, 2006).

27. Daniel Rogov, "Iraqi Cuisine," *Jewish Virtual Library,* 2005, <http://www.jewishvirtuallibrary.org/jsource/Food/ iraq.html> (February 12, 2006).

Chapter 5. Early History

1. Georges Roux, *Ancient Iraq,* 3rd ed. (London: Penguin Books, 1992), p. 2.

2. U.S. Library of Congress, "Sumer, Akkad, Babylon, and Assyria," *Country Studies: Iraq,* n.d., <http://countrystudies .us/iraq/12.htm> (October 11, 2005).

3. Roux, p. 73.

4. U.S. Library of Congress, "Sumer, Akkad, Babylon, and Assyria."

5. Ibid.

6. Ibid.

7. Lee Krystek, "The Hanging Gardens of Babylon," *Museum of Unnatural Mystery,* 1998, <http://www.unmuseum.org/hangg.htm> (October 11, 2005).

8. Alaa K. Ashmawy, "The Hanging Gardens of Babylon," *University of South Florida Department of Civil and Environmental Engineering,* January 21, 2004, <http://ce.eng.usf.edu/pharos/wonders/gardens.html> (October 11, 2005).

9. II Chronicles 22:3, *The New English Bible* (New York: Oxford University Press, 1971), p. 519.

10. U.S. Library of Congress, "Sumer, Akkad, Babylon, and Assyria."

11. U.S. Library of Congress, "The Sunni-Shia Controversy," *Country Studies: Iraq,* n.d., <http://countrystudies.us/iraq/15.htm> (October 13, 2005).

12. Ibid.

13. U.S. Library of Congress, "The Abbasid Caliphate," *Country Studies: Iraq,* n.d. <http://countrystudies.us/iraq/16.htm> (October 13, 2005).

14. U.S. Library of Congress, "The Mongol Invasion," *Country Studies: Iraq,* n.d., <http://countrystudies.us/iraq/17.htm> (October 13, 2005).

15. U.S. Library of Congress, "The Ottoman Period," *Country Studies: Iraq,* n.d., <http://countrystudies.us/iraq/18.htm> (October 14, 2005).

16. Charles Tripp, *A History of Iraq* (Cambridge: Cambridge University Press, 2001), p. 8.

Chapter 6. Modern History

1. Charles Tripp, *A History of Iraq* (Cambridge: Cambridge University Press, 2001), p. 8

2. Ibid., p. 30.

3. U.S. Library of Congress, "World War I and the British Mandate," *Country Studies: Iraq,* n.d., <http://countrystudies.us/iraq/19.htm> (October 16, 2005).

4. U.S. Library of Congress, "Iraq As an Independent Monarchy," *Country Studies: Iraq,* <http://countrystudies.us/iraq/20.htm> (October 17, 2005).

5. U.S. Library of Congress, "Republican Iraq," *Country Studies: Iraq,* n.d., <http://countrystudies.us/iraq/21.htm> (October 18, 2005).

6. "Torture, Failed Wars Left Millions Dead," *The Herald: International Edition,* October 19, 2005, p. 3A.

7. Tore Kjeilen, "Iraq: History," *Encyclopedia of the Orient,* 1996–2006, <http://i-cias.com/e.o/iraq_5.htm> (October 19, 2005).

8. Ibid., pp. 252–253.

9. Ibid., p. 253.

10. Matt Welch, "The Politics of Dead Children," *reasononline,* March 2002, <http://www.reason.com/0203/fe.mw.the.shtml> (October 24, 2005).

11. Tripp, p. 26.

12. Edith M. Lederer, "Report: Firms Paid Kickbacks to Iraq," *The Miami Herald: International Edition,* October 28, 2005, p. 1.

13. Borgna Brunner, ed., "Iraq Timeline," *infoplease,* 2005, <http://www.infoplease.com/spot/iraqtimeline1.html> (October 24, 2005).

14. Borgna Brunner, ed., "Iraq Timeline: 2002–Present," *infoplease,* 2005, <http://www.infoplease.com/spot/iraqtimeline2.html> (October 24, 2005).

15. George W. Bush, "Iraq: Denial and Deception," *The White House,* January 28, 2003, <http://www.whitehouse.gov/news/releases/2003/01/20030128-23.html> (October 24, 2005).

16. Kjeilen, "Iraq: History."

17. Colum Lynch, "U.S., Allies Dispute Annan on Iraq War," *The Washington Post,* September 17, 2004, <http://www.washingtonpost.com/wp-dyn/articles/A25685-2004Sep16.html> (October 11, 2005).

18. Sarah Anderson, et al., "IPS Releases Report on U.S. Arm-twisting Over Iraq War," *Information Clearing House,* February 26, 2003, <http://www.informationclearinghouse.info/article1740.htm> (October 11, 2005).

19. Brunner, "Iraq Timeline: 2002–Present."

Chapter 7. Iraq in Transition

1. Rick Montgomery, "Saddam Hussein's Legacy, Torture, Failed Wars Left Millions Dead," *The Miami Herald: International Edition,* October 19, 2005, p. 3A.

2. Ibid.

3. "2003: Saddam Statue Topples With Regime," *bbc.co.uk,* 2005, <http://news.bbc.co.uk/onthisday/hi/dates/stories/april/9/newsid_3502000/3502633.stm> (October 26, 2005).

4. Pat Kneisler, "Iraq Coalition Casualty Count," *icasualties.org,* 2003–2006, <http://icasualties.org/oif/default.aspx> (February 12, 2006).

5. Steven R. Hurst, "Bombing Deaths Surpass 250," *The Miami Herald: International Edition,* September 18, 2005, p. 1.

6. Rob Stein, "100,000 Civilian Deaths Estimated in Iraq," *The Washington Post,* October 29, 2004, <http://www.washingtonpost.com/wp-dyn/articles/A7967-2004Oct28.html> (October 26, 2005).

7. Borgna Brunner, ed., "Iraq Timeline: 2002-Present," *infoplease,* 2005, <http://www.infoplease.com/spot/iraqtimeline2.html> (October 27, 2005).

8. "Iraqi Governing Council," *The Coalition Provisional Authority,* n.d., <http://www.cpa-iraq.org/government/governing_council.html> (October 26, 2005).

9. Brunner, "Iraq Timeline: 2002-Present."

10. Edward Wong, "Final Tally Shows Iraqi Voters Approved New Constitution," *nytimes.com,* <http://www.nytimes.com/2005/10/25/international/middleeast/25cnd-iraq.html?hp&ex=1130299200&en=8bb546c90de6e202&ei=5094&partner=homepage> (October 25, 2005).

11. Tom Lasseter and Nancy A. Youssef, "Hussein Pleads Not Guilty to Mass Killings," *The Miami Herald: International Edition,* October 20, 2005, p. 2.

Chapter 8. The Economy

1. Steve Schifferes, "Iraq's Economy Declines by Half," *BBC News,* October 10, 2003, <http://news.bbc.co.uk/2/hi/business/3181248.stm> (October 31, 2005).

2. "Country Analysis Briefs: Iraq," *Energy Information Commission,* n.d., <http://www.eia.doe.gov/emeu/cabs/iraq.html> (October 28, 2005).

3. Bathsheba Crocker, "Reconstructing Iraq's Economy," *The Washington Quarterly,* Autumn 2004, p. 80.

4. Tore Kjeilen, "Iraq: Economy," *Encyclopedia of the Orient,* 1996–2006, <http:// http://lexicorient.com/e.o/iraq_2.htm> (February 12, 2006).

5. Patrick E. Tyler, "US Plans Credit System for Sale of Goods to Iraq," *New York Times,* reposted by *Global Policy Forum,* May 27, 2003, <http://www.globalpolicy.org/security/issues/iraq/after/2003/0527credit.htm> (February 12, 2006).

6. Crocker, p. 88.

Corzine, Phyllis. *Iraq*. San Diego, Calif.: Lucent Books, 2003.

Crisp, Peter. *Mesopotamia: Iraq in Ancient Times*. New York: Enchanted Lion Books, 2004.

Hassiq, Susan M. and Laith Muhmood. *Iraq*. Tarrytown, N.Y.: Marshall Cavendish, 2003.

Rau, Dana Meachen. *Iraq*. New York: Benchmark Books, 2004.

Richie, Jason. I*raq and the Fall of Saddam Hussein*. Minneapolis, Minn.: Oliver Press, 2003.

Schafer, Christopher. *Attack in Iraq*. Edina, Minn.: Abdo Publishing Company, 2003.

Spencer, William. *Iraq: Old Land, New Nation in Conflict*. Brookfield, Conn.: Twenty First Century Books, 2000.

Taus-Bolstad, Stacy. *Iraq in Pictures*. Minneapolis, Minn.: Lerner Publishing Group, 2003.

Willet, Edward. *Iran-Iraq War*. New York: Rosen Publishing Group, 2004.

al-Windawi, Thura, and Robin Bray. *Thura's Diary: My Life in Wartime Iraq*. New York: Viking Books, 2004.

Winter, Jeanette. *The Librarian of Basra: A True Story From Iraq*. Orlando, Fla.: Harcourt Children's Books, 2005.

Young, Jeff C. *Operation Iraqi Freedom*. Berkeley Heights, N.J.: Enslow Publishers, Inc., 2003.